Bringing online video into the classroom

Bringing online video into the classroom

Jamie Keddie

OXFORD
UNIVERSITY PRESS

Great Clarendon Street, Oxford, OX2 6DP, United Kingdom

Oxford University Press is a department of the University of Oxford.
It furthers the University's objective of excellence in research, scholarship,
and education by publishing worldwide. Oxford is a registered trade
mark of Oxford University Press in the UK and in certain other countries

ISBN: 978 0 19 442156 0

Printed in China

This book is printed on paper from certified and well-managed sources

ACKNOWLEDGEMENTS

The publishers would like to thank Oxford Design and Illustrators for resupplying
the artwork on pp.16, 17, 20, 23, 28, 29, 67; Getty Images for supplying the
image on p.102; and the following sources for permission to reproduce
screenshots: pp.16, 39 Sneezing Baby Panda, Wild Candy Pty. Ltd.; p.86
29 ways to stay creative, Copyright © 2011 by Motion Graphics Studio TO-FU;
p.93 Baby Armadillo, David Werst; pp.103, 105 Home Sweet Home, CZAR.BE
(director: Joe Vanhoutteghem, DOP: Lieven Van Baelen) for Tiense Suiker
(agency: EuroFSCG Belgium); p.106 Fresh Guacamole, © PES.

The author would like to thank the Oxford University Press team: Nick Bullard,
Ann Hunter, Julia Bell, Sophie Rogers, Robert McLarty, and Keith Layfield;
his talented video subjects: Jack Keddie, James Copeland, Jessica Lewis, Rollo
Reeder, Jamie Zhang, Andrew Foster, Julietta Schoenmann, Jodie Zhang,
Ranin Qarada, Rubén Febrero Quintairos, Kelly Jiang, Marianna Wysocki,
and Josep Casulleras; his colleagues: Derek, Gavin, Susi, Claudia, Sean, and
Kevin; Michèle Besch for her culinary art; James Thomas and Thom Kiddle for
technical help; teacher Magdalena Nogal; writer Derek Sivers and animator
Roy Prol.

For Anne (my mum)

Contents

Introduction

It's Monday morning. A group of seven-year-old boys are sitting at their desks in an exclusive public school in London. They are singing *Waltzing Matilda*, a song sometimes referred to as the unofficial national anthem of Australia. Dressed in shorts, shirts, stripy ties, and V-neck sweaters, the boys don't seem to be completely at ease with the task in hand. Perhaps this has something to do with the fact that they are singing the song in Latin. Or perhaps they are apprehensive about the cameraman at the front of the classroom who is filming their performance.

This comical moment was an opening scene from a well-known 1964 British TV documentary series called *Seven Up!*, which followed the lives of 14 British children, who were chosen to represent a range of social and economic backgrounds from across the country. As well as footage from the classroom, the filmmakers included playground fights, ballet classes, and a trip to the zoo.

Seven Up! was a product of its time. It was one small part of a storytelling revolution that took place five decades before the publication of the book you are now reading. Most notably in Canada, France, and the USA, groups of filmmakers paved the way for others to capture the intimacy and immediacy of everyday life – the candid and spontaneous. They were concerned with real people and real voices; capturing stories as they unfolded; going directly to the action rather than recreating it in a studio.

The driving force behind this change was, of course, technology. And the most important overall effect of this technological change was a new generation of lightweight video cameras and recording equipment. Cameras could now go off the tripod and onto the shoulder – out of the studio and into the world. Filmmakers and producers were able follow the action, take audiences to previously inaccessible places and give them the feeling of being there. They changed the way people saw the world then. And they created the world that we look back on today.

With new technology come new possibilities. And with new possibilities come new genres, new aesthetics, new storytelling conventions, new skills to master, new competencies to acquire, new challenges, new problems, new attitudes, new responsibilities, new ethical considerations, and new laws.

If any of this sounds familiar, perhaps that is because we are currently experiencing another storytelling revolution in which many of these changes are echoed. Back then, however, the changes involved 16 mm film and applied to a relatively small number of professionals or amateur enthusiasts. Today, they involve digital video and apply to virtually anyone who has ever owned a smart phone or webcam.

The online video age has resulted from the universal availability of video-recording devices and broadband internet connections. To a certain extent, its relatively short existence can be marked by the emergence of (at the time of writing) the third most trafficked site on the internet – YouTube.

Sites like YouTube allow virtually anyone to upload their own video content for the world to view and interact with. As a result, video has reinvented itself. It has broken free of its traditional association with TV and cinema, and started to form new collocations with terms such as **user-generated**, digital, **online**, **streaming**, **uploading**, file, **viral**, and YouTube.

Despite its relative infancy, online video culture has affected the established media, the entertainment industry, public relations, business, politics, and education in diverse and unpredictable ways.

Consider the unprecedented legacy of *Gangnam Style*, a music video by South Korean pop star, Psy. Just months after its July 2012 upload to YouTube, there was virtually no corner of human civilization that it hadn't reached. Never in the history of the world has an artefact of popular culture spread so far so quickly.

Much of the reason for the success of such a video comes from the possibility for online interaction. YouTube, for example, is host to literally millions of creative videos which reference, parody, recreate, or react to the original *Gangnam Style* video in one way or another. In the words of a young British video blogger, 'If TV is a monologue, online video is a dialogue'.

As well as introducing us to new phenomena, video-sharing culture has given rise to new art genres, new advertising techniques, and most importantly for us, new possibilities for teachers.

This book aims to address and explore these possibilities. It considers video in its reinvented form – as an accessible and interactive medium for expression.

We will look at ways of maximizing student interaction with the medium. We will suggest ways in which it can be used as a resource for language input and language study. We will see how a single engaging video can be used as a springboard not just for speaking and writing, but also as a model for students to produce and share videos of their own. And finally, we will deal with the relevant technical, practical, social, and legal considerations along the way.

Within the book, we will refer to a large number of online videos to illustrate ideas and demonstrate principles. All of these can be accessed through the following accompanying website: www.oup.com/elt/teacher/itc

Happy reading and viewing!

Part 1   Components and competencies

1 Hardware

In this first part of the book, we look at some basic skills that are necessary for any teacher who wishes to work with online video.

Of course, technology is constantly changing and there is no substitute for learning by doing or learning by watching. But our primary aims here are to demonstrate possibilities and to offer solutions to common problems.

In some cases, you will need to carry out further research and training. For this, the following resources are highly recommended.

Other teachers: The staffroom is a great place for informal learning. There is sometimes at least one teacher who is head and shoulders above the others in terms of technological knowhow. Such individuals can be invaluable. Take advantage of their expertise and pay them generously with coffee and chocolate.

Young people: It is difficult to find a teenager who has never created and shared a video clip online. Online video is so often a fundamental part of their lives. Make use of your students or your own children to teach you the tricks of the trade.

Video sites: A site like YouTube is host to a huge number of videos which demonstrate how to sew on a button, make the perfect cup of tea, or tap dance. There are also 'How to' videos for virtually any standard technological problem or query you may have. Try searching for 'How to connect a computer to a television set', 'How to change the lamp in your **projector**', or 'How to embed a video clip into your blog'.

Microsoft, Apple, and other software manufacturers often make use of instructional videos to demonstrate how to use their own products (Windows Movie Maker and iMovie, for example). Finally, you can take advantage of specialist instructional video sites for educators, such as TeacherTrainingVideos (see Appendix 8).

Online forums: As well as turning to video sites for answers, try typing your query into a standard search engine. There are many online forums where you can find answers to specific questions.

Instruction manuals: If the instruction manual for your classroom projector has been thrown away, try looking for an online version. Type the exact model of your machine into a search engine along with the words 'instruction manual'.

↓ THE PERFECT CLASSROOM

As teachers, we need to know how to make the most of the technology that we have, and how best to survive without that which we would like.

We are going to start by examining the individual components and devices necessary for bringing video into the classroom. For each one, we consider the ideal equipment and teaching conditions. We will then consider how to make the most of the circumstances which may be more familiar to many of us.

↓ THE TEACHER'S COMPUTER

Our perfect classroom would be equipped with a reliable computer, powerful enough to handle large video files without problems. It would be up-to-date, with video-related programs and applications (Adobe Flash player, for example, which is required by a lot of online video websites). If the computer wasn't up-to-date, you would have administrator's access and would be able to run installations without the need to contact the person in charge of the school's IT.

In fact, in our perfect world, the classroom computer would serve only as a backup device. You would have your own tablet computer or laptop which could be used to prepare lessons at home and brought into the classroom each day.

Such personalization is considered essential by many. By taking your own device into the classroom, you put yourself less at the mercy of the unknown, the unpredictable, the unforeseeable. Consider how well you know your own computer – you know where everything is or at least how to find it. Consider how convenient it is to have access to your own settings, your own bookmarks, or your own files. Now consider all of the potential unwelcome surprises that a communal computer can throw at you: it uses a browser that you are not used to; it refuses to recognize the video file on the memory stick that you have brought into class; you forget the logon password.

In an ideal world, we would all have our own tablets or laptops which we would take to work every day. We would walk into our classrooms, take them out of our bags and connect them to the projector and audio system. Taking comfort in the familiarity of the technology would allow us to relax and do our jobs better. This is the beauty of technological personalization.

↓ DISPLAYING VIDEO IN THE CLASSROOM

Ideally, we would be able to connect our computers or mobile devices to a wall- or ceiling-mounted digital projector. The projector would have two inputs – one for the permanent classroom computer, and another for your own device.

The projector would have a good resolution and contrast ratio so projected images would be sharp and clear. Colour production would be excellent – reds would be reds, and greens would be greens. Importantly, the projector would have a light output perfectly suited to the classroom so it would never

Hardware

be necessary to block out natural light and turn the classroom into a cinema. Also, it would probably be a 'short throw' projector – that is, one that can be mounted a few metres away from the screen and, therefore, doesn't shine in the user's eyes. And, of course, the projector would be silent – no distracting hums or buzzes!

FIGURE 1.1   *An ideal classroom for video projection*

The screen itself could be a standard whiteboard or an **interactive whiteboard**. Both of these would allow the teacher or students to get creative and combine projected images with handwritten text and hand-drawn objects.

IMAGE 1.1   *A whiteboard combining video and handwritten text*

As well as the big screen, there would be a perfect audio system: a wall-mounted speaker system capable of producing crisp sound at volume levels which can reach everyone in the classroom. There would be no annoying background hiss from the speakers to distract teacher or learners.

There are other dream possibilities of course. I have seen schools which equip their classrooms with large wall-mounted flat screen televisions connected to computers.

However, in reality, many of us will be dependent on communal portable equipment which we have to reserve and set up in the classroom 15 minutes before the lesson begins. Although less convenient, this is better than having no big-screen display option at all.

✓ *Getting it right*

Connecting a PC to a projector

LCD projectors are probably the most common type to be found in schools. As is the case for most computer monitors and high definition television sets, the standard way of connecting an LCD projector to a computer is through an analogue **VGA** cable.

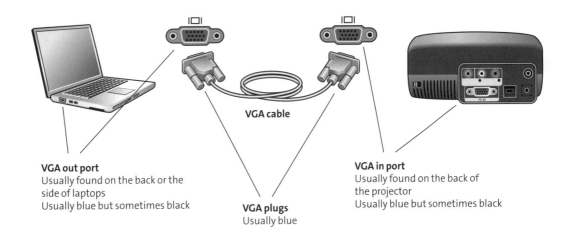

VGA cable

VGA out port
Usually found on the back or the side of laptops
Usually blue but sometimes black

VGA plugs
Usually blue

VGA in port
Usually found on the back of the projector
Usually blue but sometimes black

FIGURE 1.2   *A projector, a VGA cable, and a computer.*

Once in place, the screws at the side of the plug should be tightened gently. Note that you should not plug or unplug a VGA cable unless both the computer and projector are switched off.
When the computer and projector are connected and turned on, the projected image may appear automatically. If not, you will have to make use of the 'display select' function key on your keyboard. The specific key that you want will depend on your computer model but it will often be either F4, F5, F7, or F8. It might also be labelled with a small icon which looks like a computer screen or the letters LCD/CRT. To activate the function key, you may have to press it while holding down the Fn key (usually located at the bottom left of the keyboard). Once you have done this, the projector should pick up the signal and the computer display should be beamed through the projector.

Hardware

As this happens, your computer screen may go blank. If this is the case, activate the function key a second time – for many computers, the display select function key moves between three modes: computer screen display only; projector screen display only; computer and projector screen display together.

There may be further details specific to the machines that you are working with, and you may have to consult the instruction manual or a colleague. Experiment with the distance between the projector and screen – the closer the projector to the screen, the smaller, but brighter, the image will be. Focus the image on the screen using the ring, dial, or switch on the projector.

Note that VGA cables transfer images but not sound. The classroom audio system must be connected directly to your computer.

 **Getting it right**

Connecting a Mac to a projector

Some computers – most notably Macs – have no standard VGA port. The alternatives include the Mini-VGA, the Mini-DVI, and the Mini DisplayPort. In such cases, an adaptor will be required to connect the computer to a VGA cable and then to a projector. Once connected, the projector should pick up the signal automatically.

IMAGE 1.2   *A MacBook Pro connected to a VGA cable via an adaptor*

Getting it right

Connecting a tablet computer to a projector

Many tablet computers, such as the iPad, contain a single connector for power and data transfer. Such devices require model-specific VGA adaptors in order to connect to standard projectors. Fortunately, an increasing number of presenters are working from mobile devices and as a result, such adaptors are not usually difficult to find. Once connected, the projector should automatically pick up the signal for most mobile devices.

Note that some tablet computers cannot be connected to a projector and mains power at the same time. Make sure that your device is fully charged before coming to class.

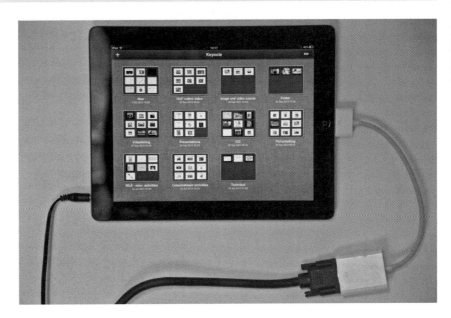

IMAGE 1.3   *A tablet computer connected to a VGA cable via an adaptor*

✓ *Getting it right*

Connecting a computer to a television set

In the absence of a projector, a standard high-definition television set might be a viable alternative. Perhaps your school or teaching venue has a TV on wheels that can be moved between rooms. A laptop, a tablet computer, or an iPod can be connected to the TV, which in turn, can be used as a monitor for communal viewing. Again, for this purpose, a VGA connection is required. As is the case with connecting a PC to a projector (see above), you will have to find out which function key to switch between displays once the computer and TV set are turned on.

Hiding the projected image

In Part 3, we will look at ideas for activities in which students listen to video without seeing the screen. There are a several ways to hide a projected image:

- Look for the function on the projector remote control that allows you to temporarily hide the projected image. The button may be labelled as *blank*, *no show*, *black screen*, or *hide*.
- For PCs, make use of the 'display select' function key on your computer keyboard (see page 17 Getting it right: Connecting a PC to a projector).
- Convert a video file to an MP3 file (audio only). We will see how to do this in the next chapter.
- Physically disconnect your device from the projector. This is cumbersome but may work as a last resort when none of the above are possible.

Poor quality projector images

A typical projector lamp has about 2,000 to 3,000 hours of life. After that time, the image starts to lose its brightness and you need to get a replacement lamp module.

A short-term solution is to move the projector closer to the screen. This will increase the brightness, but reduce the size of the image. Another more traditional method is to block out sunlight coming in through the windows and thus turn the classroom into a cinema. Some teenagers may prefer this!

It is always worth experimenting with the projector controls (brightness, contrast, etc.) to make sure that you have the optimum settings.

Poor quality audio system

There is currently a huge range of powerful, cheap, pocket-sized speakers that can be connected directly to computers or mobile devices. Most of these require charging via a **USB**-to-computer connection. This is no problem if used with laptops, which generally have USB ports. However, this is not the case for many tablet computers and other mobile devices. In such cases, ensure that the speakers are charged before bringing them into the classroom.

No big screen for displaying video in the classroom

Sometimes, a small screen is sufficient for communal video viewing, even for fairly large groups. As long as the video clip is short, and as long as the activity doesn't require students to pay attention to small visual details, then a laptop or tablet computer screen may be enough.

Prior to viewing, ask students to stand up and get into formation as if you were going to take a class photograph. Stand in front of them with your device in hand and show the video. If you feel self-conscious, place the computer on a table.

FIGURE 1.3   *A group of students watching a video in front of a tablet computer*

Alternatively, activities can be designed so that video viewing takes place on students' own devices either in, or out of the classroom. Note, however, that a small screen and high frequency audio can severely reduce the experience of viewing videos on smartphones.

Finally, it is worth pointing out that pocket projectors may, one day soon, become a practical and economical option for displaying video in the classroom. However, at the time of writing, although small enough to fit into handbags, they are generally expensive and have low light outputs.

↓ INTERNET ACCESS

In our perfect teaching word, our schools would all be equipped with wireless broadband connections which are fast, reliable, and never go down. Video websites and online applications would work seamlessly. For example, there would be none of those frustrating moments when a streamed video clip refuses to play or decides to get stuck half-way through viewing.

With access to laptops or tablet computers in the classroom, students can get online instantly, without the need to leave the classroom to go to a designated computer room. In other words, instead of planning the week according to online and offline time (which requires advance bookings of the computer room), teachers would know that their students have online access whenever they needed it, or whenever their work required it.

In cases when students use their own devices, they should have access to the school network password and should not be expected to connect to 3G or other wireless networks which would potentially be quite expensive.

Technology is becoming increasingly mobile. The traditional designated computer room will gradually become a thing of the past. In order for schools to take advantage of the possibilities, wireless broadband connections are essential.

No internet in the classroom

There are a number of ways of playing video in the classroom without online access and these are discussed in the next chapter.

↓ THE STUDENTS' DEVICES

Of course, in a world of wishes, all of our learners would be responsible, motivated individuals. There would be no need to put blocks on video websites. Learners could be trusted to work at computers without playing their favourite music videos as soon as the teacher's back is turned. We would not have to stop students bringing their mobile phones into the classroom. In fact, we would actively encourage it and integrate such devices into the activities that we plan.

Just like their teacher, students would have access to the same technology in the classroom as they do at home. Each day, they would bring in their own laptops, tablet computers, or smartphones which would all have inbuilt **video cameras**.

Students' devices would be up to date with the essential video apps and video tools for educational purposes. Students would be able to watch, create, edit, and upload video either collaboratively or individually. They would be able to add subtitles to videos, write comments on videos, **embed** videos in a class **virtual learning environment** (VLE) or other online space (see next chapter). They would be able to connect with other English learners or English speakers in other parts of the world through video chat applications.

Distracted students

Mobile phones can be incredibly distracting at the best of times and notoriously problematic in the classroom. Understandably, many schools ban them from their premises altogether.

On the other hand, a mobile device can be a powerful and motivating learning tool. And taking advantage of students' own technology whenever possible would seem to make practical and economic sense.

This book offers a number of suggestions for activities which make use of mobile devices in the hands of the learners. Different teachers who embrace these technologies will have different approaches and techniques for maximizing efficiency and minimizing distraction.

Try this ☞ **Incorporating smartphones into video activities**

1   Start the lesson by telling your students that they will be making use of their smartphones. This knowledge alone can be quite motivating, especially for learners who are not used to such an approach.
2   Ask everyone to take out their devices and make sure that they are switched to silent or 'do not disturb' mode.
3   Ask everyone to place their phones on a specially-designated area – a table at the front of the classroom, for example. All phones should now be out of reach of their owners. The class can now take place as planned without any technological interference and meanwhile, student curiosity is maintained.
4   Later, when the phones are required, invite students to take them back and complete the video task that you have set.
5   Give a time limit. Insist that all devices have to be returned to the designated area after 15 minutes, for example.

↓ VIDEO-RECORDING DEVICES

Camcorders, digital cameras, smartphones, tablet computers, and video glasses can be incorporated into a huge range of language learning tasks and activities. In our dream school, all learners would have access to simple video-recording devices, both in and out of the classroom.

In some situations, this may already be a reality: many of us carry smartphones with us wherever we go, and the same can be said for many students. These devices are equipped with simple, yet perfectly adequate video-recording functions. Smartphones and mobile devices in general are sometimes regarded as the perfect video tools for the classroom. The big attraction is that they serve as all-in-one devices. Students can use them to create, edit, and share video without the need to transfer files from one device to another. This is a major advantage of using mobile devices for video creation.

Transferring video files

Unlike mobile devices, camcorders and digital cameras must be connected to a computer for video file transfer after filming. The most common ways to do this are:

- Remove the **SD** card from the camera and insert it directly into an SD card slot on a computer (if it has one).
- Insert the SD card into a reader and then connect the reader to a USB port on a computer.
- Via a USB arm. This is a feature that was associated with a range of mini camcorders such as the Flip, Kodak Play, and Sony Bloggie. However, most cameras of this type are now out of production.
- Via a USB cable.

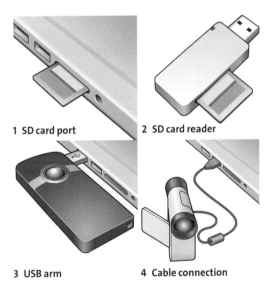

1 SD card port   2 SD card reader

3 USB arm   4 Cable connection

FIGURE I.4   *Four computer connection possibilities*

Although transferring a video file to a computer is not a complicated process in itself, it can be a potentially awkward and time-consuming step when there is more than one camera involved.

Imagine you are working with a group of 16 students. As part of a speaking activity, you have presented them with a problem and put them into four groups of four to solve it. The task is for students to share ideas and reach a consensus solution. Once this has been done, you give out four video cameras – one to each group. A spokesperson from each group then has to present their group's solution to the camera. What do you do next?

Whatever you plan to do with the resulting video clips, they have to be transferred from the cameras to a computer. The question is, who does this and when? Here are three possibilities:

Try this ☞ **The teacher does it**

If you are just dealing with four video files, then the transfer shouldn't require too much work. But any more than that, and the work starts to mount up, especially if you also have to upload and share the clips as well. One piece of advice is to delete all videos from the cameras before giving them out to students, and ask students to delete any unwanted videos before giving them back to you. Like actors, students may require more than one 'take' in order to get the result that they want in front of the camera. Identifying video clips which are generated from such false starts can be time consuming for the teacher.

Try this ☞ **The computer room**

In situations involving more cameras and multiple video files, it's a better option to get the students to do the work. A school computer room is the ideal place to transfer clips to computers, edit them if necessary, and share them with the rest of the group. Students could do this 15 minutes before the end of the lesson. Bear in mind that unless you have one camera per student (generally impractical and unnecessary) not everyone will be involved in this process and students without cameras will require something else to do.

Try this ☞ **Students take cameras home**

This is, of course, the natural option if students are making use of their own cameras, but a risky last resort if the cameras belong to the school or the teacher. Perhaps students could take home the memory cards only. A lost memory card would be easier to replace than a lost video camera. However, memory cards are delicate and must be protected.

Incompatible file problems

As a general rule, the simpler the camera, the better suited it is to the classroom. The more complex the device, the more there is to go wrong. Imagine you are using a video camera that you have never used before. Later, you transfer the video file to your computer only to find that the file won't open or play – it is incompatible with your machine.

Cameras that are capable of creating high definition (HD) video sometimes use unusual file types which are not recognized without specialist software. If you don't know your video camera well, then it is recommended that you switch to standard definition (SD) mode if possible. SD files are usually more widely recognized. More information about different file types is given in the next chapter.

2   Software

Less than ten years ago, teachers who used video in the classroom were at the mercy of the material. Access was limited to the DVDs or VHS tapes in staffrooms or private collections, and we were largely unable to personalize and adapt the medium for our learners and for the activities that we intended to create.

Nowadays, the software really is soft: you can chop it up; put it back together; change the audio; add your own subtitles. Perhaps most importantly, anyone can now create their own video content and share it with the world.

In order to become video creators and manipulators, there are a number of fundamental skills to acquire and these are discussed in this chapter.

↓ VIDEO FILES

Just as there are different types of document files (DOC, DOCX, PAGES, PDF, HTML, CSV, etc.) so there are many different types of video file, such as:

File	Full name	Associated with	Compatibility
MP4	MPEG-4	Apple	Most devices and applications, especially Macs and Mac applications.
MOV	QuickTime File Format	Apple	Apple devices and applications
AVI	Audio Video Interleave	Microsoft	Most devices and applications, especially PCs and PC applications.
WMV	Windows Media Video	Microsoft	Most devices and applications especially PCs and PC applications.
FLV	Flash Video	Adobe	Often requires a special FLV player.

TABLE 2.1   *Common examples of video files*

Different file types have different properties and functions. However, in many situations, you don't need to worry. For example, if a user uploads a video onto a video-sharing website, the file may be converted to an FLV file automatically, without the user's knowledge.

Problems usually arise when you transfer video files from one device to another. Consider the following situation: a student creates a short video on her smartphone and then transfers the video file to a school computer. It played perfectly on her smartphone, but the school computer doesn't recognize the video file and refuses to open or play it.

This situation would have been avoided if the student had uploaded and shared the video directly from her own device – the smartphone. Mobile

Software

devices, in general, can be regarded as all-in-one tools for filming, editing, and uploading. For this reason, they are an increasingly attractive option for teachers interested in classroom video projects.

Sometimes, however, transferring video files will be unavoidable. For example, it is often necessary to transfer a video file from a camcorder to a computer, or take a video file into class on a memory stick. In such cases, it is essential to know what type of video files the recipient machine is capable of working with.

✓ *Getting it right*

VLC player

The very useful VLC player is a free multimedia player that plays the vast majority of video files (see Appendix 7). So, for example, a Mac computer which has the VLC player installed will be able to play AVI and WMV files (see Table on page 25).

✓ *Getting it right*

Converting a video file from one type to another

Zamzar is a good video file converter which is free and simple to use (see Appendix 7). As an online application, you will have to upload your video file, select the new format that you want and provide your email address so that a link to the new video file can be sent to you. Zamzar is useful for converting video files to MP3 files (audio only). This can be useful for activities in which students hear a video without seeing the screen. We will see ideas for such activities in Part 3.

↓ VIDEO-EDITING APPLICATIONS

Video-editing tools can be thought of as digital scissors and glue for video files. They can be used to cut up video, isolate parts of it, delete unwanted parts, create a montage of different clips, remove audio, add music, add subtitles, and more.

The best-known video-editing software applications are probably Windows Movie Maker for PCs and iMovie for Mac devices. But there are many other possibilities including online applications, and also video-editing apps for mobile devices (see Appendix 7). One of the best ways to learn how to use a video-editing application it to search for instructional videos online.

Let's look at an example of what can be done with a video-editing application. Video 2.1 has not been edited (see our accompanying website: www.oup.com/elt/teacher/itc). It is the raw footage. Watch it and consider what editing changes you might want to make.

Now watch Video 2.2. This is the edited version. Look out for the changes that were made.

Many video-editing principles, functions, and items of terminology are standard, regardless of the application that is used. In order to make edits like the ones demonstrated in the previous clip, you need to investigate the specific application that you want to use and find out how to perform simple functions such as:

- Create a new project
- Import video into a video-editing application
- Split a clip
- Delete a clip
- Add text
- Add a transition
- Export video.

There are generally four steps to a standard editing job: creating a project, importing the media, making the edits, and exporting the new video. We will take these one at a time.

Step 1: creating a new project

Regardless of the simplicity or complexity of the task, everything you do on a video-editing application has to be done in a project. A project may involve one simple edit to a single video file. Or it may involve combining a whole series of shots together and adding audio files to create a short film.

Once you have created a new project, you will have to give it a name. As you will see from the diagram below, I called mine: *Shooting on a mobile device*.

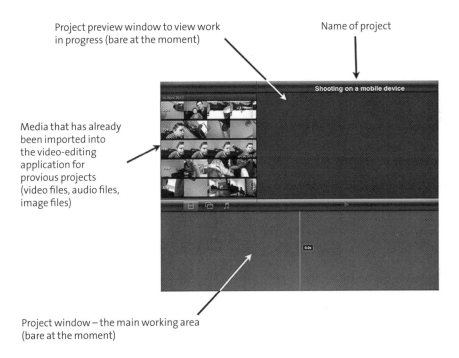

Project preview window to view work in progress (bare at the moment)

Name of project

Media that has already been imported into the video-editing application for provious projects (video files, audio files, image files)

Project window – the main working area (bare at the moment)

FIGURE 2.1   *A standard video-editing application showing a new project*

 **Getting it right**

Aspect ratio and frame rate

If, when creating a project, your video-editing application asks you to specify the aspect ratio and frame rate, choose the default options in both cases. Aspect ratio refers to the screen dimensions and the most common ones are 4:3 (usually the default standard) and 16:9 (widescreen). Frame rate refers to the number of images or frames that play per second. This generally depends on the video-recording device rather than the video file. For example, most camcorders purchased in the USA record at 30 fps (frames per second) while those purchased in Europe record at 25 fps.

Software

Step 2: importing the media

The media are the raw ingredients for the project. In my project, there were three ingredients – the raw video and two photographs. Other projects could also involve audio files (music, for example).

Depending on the device that you use, there are three potential steps to complete in order to get the media into your video-editing application. These are shown in the following diagram.

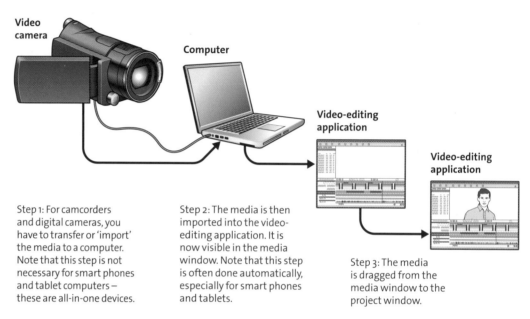

Step 1: For camcorders and digital cameras, you have to transfer or 'import' the media to a computer. Note that this step is not necessary for smart phones and tablet computers – these are all-in-one devices.

Step 2: The media is then imported into the video-editing application. It is now visible in the media window. Note that this step is often done automatically, especially for smart phones and tablets.

Step 3: The media is dragged from the media window to the project window.

FIGURE 2.2   *From video camera to video editor*

After dragging the video into the project window, the video-editing application may now look something like this:

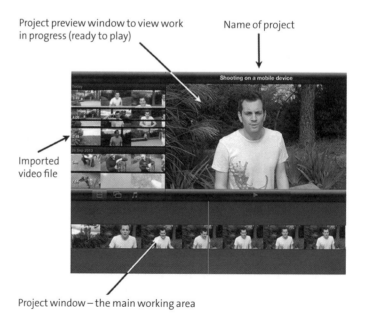

Project preview window to view work in progress (ready to play)

Name of project

Imported video file

Project window – the main working area

FIGURE 2.3   *A standard video-editing application with video in project browser*

Note that the video clip is displayed as a timeline – a series of thumbnail images placed side by side. This can be regarded as a piece of tape waiting to be cut up. In the above image, the timeline can be seen in the project window – the workbench of the video-editing application; the place where it all happens.

 **Getting it right**

From recording device to editing application

It is often possible to import a video clip directly from a video-recording device to a video-editing application. This is certainly the case when filming and editing on mobile devices. Any video that is filmed using a tablet computer, for example, will generally be imported automatically to any video-editing app that has been installed on the same device.

Step 3: making the edits

I made the following edits to my original video file:

Edit	Function(s) to look for
Included text at the beginning.	Add **text** or **titles**
Removed a number of parts of the video (redundant sections or moments when I made mistakes). Note that the edited version is 40 seconds shorter than the unedited version.	**Split** and **delete**
Inserted transitions (e.g. the fades at the beginning and end, the dissolve at 1:40).	Add **transition/fade in/fade out**
Included two non-moving images.	**Import** image file
Included credits.	Add **text** or **titles**
Increased the volume.	Make **audio** adjustments or edits

TABLE 2.2   *Editing functions to look for*

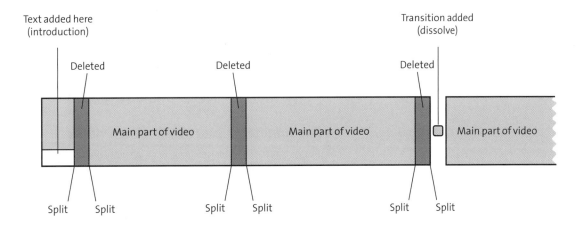

FIGURE 2.4   *A timeline showing some edits*

Software

As mentioned above, you will have to become familiar with your own video-editing application and learn how to apply these functions.

Step 4: exporting or uploading the new video

Once you are happy with the edits that you have made, the final step is to export the new video. This will convert the project into a new video file.

The new video file can either be exported onto your computer or directly onto a video-sharing site such as YouTube.

Once uploaded onto YouTube, I was able to add subtitles using the Captions function and add an onscreen note using the Annotations function (Appendix 4).

↓ SUBTITLES

There are two types of subtitles that are associated with online video: closed (or hard) and open (or soft).

Closed (or hard) subtitles

These are subtitles that are added directly to the video, using a video-editing application. They cannot be turned off or altered in any way. An example of such subtitles can be seen in Video 2.3 (see our accompanying website: www.oup.com/elt/teacher/itc).

Open (or soft) subtitles

Rather than adding subtitles directly to a video file, they can be added to a video which has been uploaded onto a site like YouTube. Subtitles like this are open. That means that they can be turned on and off. Sometimes we can also switch between different languages.

An example of open subtitles can be seen on Video 2.2. By clicking on the subtitle icon underneath the video window, you will be able to turn the subtitles on and off as well as change their size, colour, and background.

Be aware of automatically generated subtitles on sites like YouTube as they are notorious for containing nonsensical English!

 *Getting it right*

Adding subtitles to your own YouTube videos

For videos that you have uploaded onto YouTube yourself, look for the *Captions* function. Select *Add captions* and then *Transcribe and sync*. For this, YouTube has an excellent function that allows you to transcribe the video, which automatically pauses whenever you are typing. Once you have finished transcribing, press *Sync*. The site will process the text and synchronize the subtitles with the audio.

Software

 *Getting it right*

Adding subtitles to other people's videos
Unfortunately, YouTube doesn't allow you to add subtitles to other people's videos but there are a number of other sites that do, such as Overstream and Subtitle-horse (see Appendix 7). However, these are slightly more complicated to use than the YouTube option discussed above.

↓ VIDEO-HOSTING SITES

Common video-hosting sites (also called video-sharing sites) include YouTube, Vimeo, and Youku (see Appendix 3). Sites like these allow users to upload their videos for others to watch. Uploading should be distinguished from **downloading**, which means to take a clip from the internet and store it on your own computer or device.

Standard computers

There are many free video-sharing sites that can be used to upload and share video content (see Appendix 3). Almost all of these will require you to register first. Once you have done so, uploading a video may mean simply logging into the website, clicking on the upload button, and then selecting the desired video file from your computer. You may even be able to drag and drop it from your computer to the browser page.

The uploading process can take some time. The larger the file, the longer it will take. Once a clip starts to upload, you can usually start to work on settings. For example, you can name it, include information about it, and choose your privacy option (discussed below).

Mobile devices

There are fewer options when uploading from mobile devices. At the time of writing, many mobile devices have a strong bias for YouTube and Vimeo (see Appendix 3).

Videos created on an iPad can be uploaded directly to YouTube. Alternatively, if you want to upload to Vimeo, you will have to download and register with the free Vimeo app (see Appendix 3). When asked to do so, you should give permission for the app to access all of your videos on the iPad. After that, you will be able to upload videos directly from the device to Vimeo.

 *Getting it right*

Uploading to YouTube from school-owned devices
For reasons of security, Google (the owner of YouTube) can make it difficult for users to sign in to a new device. This can cause unexpected technical problems in the classroom. If you are using school-owned tablet computers, prepare in the following way:
1 Make sure that your school has its own Google account.
2 Use this to log in to the YouTube app on all of the mobile devices.
3 Run a test: upload a short test video onto YouTube from two or three of the mobile devices to make sure that the process works smoothly.

 *Getting it right*

Students can have their own accounts

You might want to encourage students to register themselves with a video-sharing site. When uploading videos, they can then do so directly to their own accounts. This is more practical than using a communal account, as you will not have to share passwords. It also means that students own the content that they create. Although this means that class videos will be hosted in different places, they can all be displayed together on a VLE (virtual learning environment) or other online space (discussed later in the chapter).

Privacy

When uploading a video, you can choose from a number of privacy options which will determine who has access to your video. Different sites offer different possibilities. YouTube, for example, allows users to choose between the following three privacy settings:

1 Public. Anyone can watch the video.

2 Private. Only specific people that you choose can view the video. Unfortunately, you can only choose up to 25 people.

3 Unlisted. This is probably the most practical option. Only people who have the **URL** link to the video can watch it. The URL link consists of a complex combination of numbers, letters, and other characters, and in this way, it can be regarded as a key to your video. Anyone who has the key can share it with whoever they like, but the video cannot be found through a search.

Similarly, Vimeo has a number of privacy options including one which allows a user to password-protect an uploaded video. This means that only those with the password can view it. Students could protect their videos on the site with a communal group password chosen by yourself.

Another setting to consider when uploading videos onto YouTube is whether or not to allow others to leave comments. By default, anyone can leave comments on your videos. Teachers and students who opt for the public privacy setting on YouTube are strongly recommended to disable this option. We will speak more about this in Part 4.

↓ VIRTUAL LEARNING ENVIRONMENTS AND OTHER ONLINE SPACES

The more we create and make use of videos in and out of the classroom, the greater the need to organize them, document them, and make them accessible to students.

As a teacher, you may want to do any or all of the following:

• Share all of the videos that you use in your classroom and thus make them accessible to your students.
• Include any accompanying or supplementary materials (uploaded files, worksheets, transcripts, instructions for tasks, links to web pages, etc.)

- Share and make accessible the videos that you create yourself for the purposes of instruction, explanation, etc. (We will speak more about this in Chapter 12.)

As for students, we may want them to do the following:

- Access all videos and accompanying materials that are used in the classroom as and when required (for homework or revision, for example).
- Share the videos that they create themselves with you.
- Make their videos accessible to each other.
- Leave comments on videos.

There are many possible online spaces that can be used for these purposes. The most versatile of these is the VLE, common examples of which include Moodle and Blackboard. Setting up a VLE can be expensive and/or require expertise. Using one may require some training on the part of the teacher and students. For this reason, VLEs are usually managed at the level of the institution rather than the individual teacher. If your school has a VLE, it is certainly worth looking into the possibilities and seeking the necessary instruction.

In other situations, you may want to go alone and set up a **blog**, **wiki**, or online group for each of the classes that you teach. Appendix 5 suggests a number of free options for creating an online space on which you and your students can share videos and interact.

 *Getting it right*

Time management

Setting up and maintaining an online space requires time, effort, discipline, and the implementation of new classroom protocols. You may also have to research possibilities and train yourself and your students. Rather than setting up a blog, wiki, or online group for every class that you teach, it might be a better idea to focus on one class first and experiment from there. That way, you will get an idea of the workload and time required and learn to get organized before extending the practice to your other classes.

Link sharing

At this stage, it is essential to make a distinction between video hosting and link sharing.

Video hosting

As we saw earlier in the chapter, YouTube is an example of a video-hosting site. Uploading a video onto such a site means storing it directly on that site's server.

Link sharing

Imagine that you have found an interesting online video and you want to share it with a friend. You could do this by email, Facebook, Twitter, etc. The important thing is that you would not send the video itself. That would be

Software

cumbersome and completely unnecessary. Instead, you would send a link to the video. Your friend would then click on the link and watch the video on the host site.

It is important to understand the difference between video hosting and link sharing for one important reason: most VLEs, blogs, wikis, and similar online spaces are not video-hosting sites; they are places for sharing links.

As teachers, whenever we want to share the videos that we use in the classroom, we can quite simply share links to those videos. Similarly, if students upload their own videos onto a host site (their own YouTube account, for example) they can then share the link on a VLE or other online space.

Embedding videos

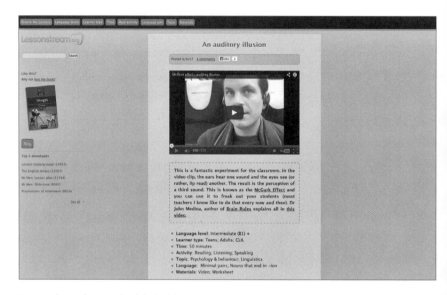

IMAGE 2.1   *Screenshot of an embedded video on Lessonstream*

The above **screenshot** shows an example of a video which is hosted on YouTube but embedded on the author's own website. This conveniently allows visitors to watch the video without the need to leave the page.

For teachers and learners who wish to share video clips, the ability to embed them on a VLE or other online space is an attractive option for the following reasons.

Less distraction

Leaving one website to visit another can easily consume precious time. Video-sharing sites, for example, tempt us with more 'related videos'. An embedded video has fewer of these distractions; it also has fewer advertisements.

Software

Visual reference

An embedded screen looks good and provides visual information about the content of the video. The alternative to an embedded video would be a hyperlink. Imagine how much more difficult it would be to scan through pages of hyperlinked text to find the video that you are looking for.

Comments

If an activity requires students to leave comments on a video, the best way to do this would be to embed the video on a VLE or other online space and ask them to leave comments directly on that page.

Try this  **Embedding a video**

In order to embed a video, a webpage will require a short piece of code (html, for example). The code provides information about where the video should come from (YouTube, Vimeo, etc.) and how big the embedded screen should appear. The code can be copied directly from the video site and pasted into your VLE, blog post, wiki page, etc. If you have some blogging experience, the process should be fairly straightforward:

1   Go to a site such as YouTube or Vimeo and find a video that you would like to embed.
2   Look for the embed button and click on it. The embed button will usually be found somewhere around the video screen. Sometimes it will be found on the screen itself. Sometimes it has to be accessed by clicking on a share button first. This depends on the video site.
3   After clicking on the embed button, you will be presented with the code. Before copying, you will probably be given some additional options, most notably, to specify the size of the embedded video screen.
4   Once you have specified the size that you would like, copy the code.
5   On your blog or wiki dashboard, paste the code into the page or post that you are writing or editing. Wordpress, and most other content management systems, have two writing modes – visual and text. Make sure that you paste the embed code into the text mode.

IMAGE 2.2   *Screenshot of an embedded code in a Wordpress dashboard*

↓ NON-HOSTING OPTIONS

In some situations, it may be undesirable for students to upload the videos that they create onto sites such as YouTube or Vimeo. If this is the case, we need to consider alternative ways of sharing video files between students and teacher, and/or students and students. Here are some possibilities:

Email

For activities which involve the creation of short videos (see the Try this activity 'Spokesperson' on page 135, for example) students could email their video files directly to you. This would allow you to open them and display them on the projector for communal viewing. However, for this to work, everyone must be aware of video file size restrictions: if a file is too large, it will not send.

Cloud sharing

A site such as Drop Box (see Appendix 7) would allow you to create a communal online folder and send invitations to all group members to join it (email addresses are needed for this). Students could then upload their video files to the folder where they could be accessed by everyone in the group.

Virtual Learning Environments

Students can upload video files onto a VLE in the same way that they would upload a Word document or other file. You could then download them as you would do for a video file attachment in an email. Note, however, that there are often restrictions on the size of files that can be uploaded.

Memory sticks

Students could submit their video files to you on memory sticks. Make sure that each stick is clearly labelled with the name of its owner. This method can get cumbersome, however, especially for larger groups.

↓ DOWNLOADING VIDEOS

There are a number of potential problems associated with playing videos online in the classroom. Here are a few of them.

Unreliable internet

Slow or inconsistent connections mean that online videos may freeze, stick, or even refuse to play at all. Some teachers may have no internet connection in their classroom.

Software

Control problems

The streaming bar underneath an online video can be clumsy to negotiate. For example, it can be difficult to find or replay a specific part of a video, even with a good internet connection. It is usually easier to control videos when we don't have to stream them (i.e. when we have them stored on our computers).

Dead links

A video clip that you planned to use in class can be removed from the internet without warning.

Potential to distract

The mere presence of a site like YouTube can be very disruptive in the classroom. Many of us will be familiar with students attempting to persuade the teacher to play their favourite clips rather than focus on the video task in hand. This can be particularly problematic at the end of a video, when suggested links to other videos are given.

Advertisements

Videos can be associated with advertisements that are inappropriate for the classroom.

Unwanted titles

The activity that we plan may depend on students not knowing the title of a video. For example, if we wanted to use a video for a 'what happens next?' activity, we would not want students to see the words *Sneezing baby panda* at the top of the screen. However, it can be awkward or even impossible to hide video titles on certain video sites.

Offline options

You can overcome all of these problems if you download a video from its host site so that it can be stored on your computer and played without an internet connection. Here are some ideas:

- Some video websites will allow you to download videos as video files, rename them if necessary, and store them on your computer hard drives (see Appendix 1). You can then take your laptop into class or transfer a video file to a classroom computer via a memory stick. Either option will allow you to play the video in class without online access.
- Some video apps will allow you to select specific clips for **offline** viewing (see Appendix 1). This will benefit teachers who take their own mobile devices into the classroom.

- There are a number of online applications, browser **plugins**, and mobile apps that allow users to download or 'capture' online video clips such as Savevid, Downloadhelper, and Torch (see Appendix 7). Please note, however, that users should check with individual video sites before capturing their videos, as doing so may constitute a breach of copyright and terms of service.

✓ *Getting it right* **Subtitles**

A downloaded video will lose its open (or soft) subtitles. For this reason, downloading a video might not be an option if you intend to make use of its subtitles.

✓ *Getting it right* **Using SafeShare**

Some of the previously-mentioned problems can be avoided with Safeshare (see Appendix 7). Find a YouTube video that you would like to use, copy the URL address, and paste it into the window at Safeshare. You can then generate a link to a video which is free from the distraction of advertisements, comments, and video suggestions. The site also gives teachers the possibility to rename the video. It works well on standard computers as well as mobile devices. Another way of avoiding the distractions of online videos is to embed and play them in a Prezi presentation (see Appendix 7).

↓ ORGANIZING AND PLAYING VIDEO FILES

With a collection of video files on your computer you will want to keep them organized so that you can find what you want as quickly and efficiently as possible.

One excellent way of doing this is to make use of media players. Applications such as iTunes and Windows Media Player can be used to organize and play the video files that are stored on a computer hard drive. Videos can be organized into playlists according to date, content, teaching purpose, etc. And of course, media players can be synchronized across different devices so that the video library on your laptop can be simply transferred to your tablet computer, smartphone, or iPod.

For teachers and students who wish to incorporate video into multimedia slideshows, presentation programs will be useful. Video can easily be embedded into presentations created on Microsoft PowerPoint, Apple Keynote, or Prezi (see Appendix 7).

↓ SCREENSHOTS

A screenshot or screen capture is essentially a photograph of your computer screen. The ability to take screenshots allows us to obtain stills (non-moving images) from online video clips.

In order to generate a still from a video, you will have to play the video on full screen mode, pause it at the key moment, and then take the screenshot.

✓ *Getting it right*

How to take a screenshot on a PC computer

There is a button located at the top right hand side of PC keyboards which says Print Screen or PrtScrn. Press this once and you will copy the display that you see on your screen. You will then have to paste the image into another program such as Microsoft Paint or PowerPoint.

IMAGE 2.3   *A still from a video clip: 'Sneezing Baby Panda – The Movie'*

✓ *Getting it right*

How to take a screenshot on a Mac computer

To capture the whole screen, press and hold down shift, then command and then 3. An image file containing the screenshot will immediately appear on your desktop. In order to capture a part of the screen, press and hold down shift, command and then 4 and click and drag over the specific area that you want to capture.

✓ *Getting it right*

How to take a screenshot on a mobile device

Mobile devices usually require that a combination of buttons are pressed simultaneously. For example, for the iPad, the menu button and the power button must be pressed at the same time. The screen shot can then be found in the photos app.

Screenshot applications

Rather than using the built-in function on your computer, you may prefer to use a screenshot application or app. There are many available. One of the best known of these is Jing (see Appendix 7) which also allows text to be added to the resulting images.

↓ SCREENCASTS

If screenshots are essentially photographs of your computer screen, then **screencasts** are videos. Instructional videos that demonstrate onscreen technological skills (how to use video-editing applications, how to navigate websites, or how to embed videos into a PowerPoint presentation) make use of screencast software.

As well as recording your computer screen, screencast software also records your voice. This means that screencast software can be an effective tool, especially if you work in blended learning or flipped classroom contexts (see page 149). Some educators are enthusiastic about the possibilities for using screencasts to provide students with running commentary feedback on their written assignments.

There are a number of free screencast software applications and mobile apps available, such as Jing and CamStudio (see Appendix 7). Mac users can make use of QuickTime Player which has its own screencast function (open QuickTime Player, go to File, and select New Screen Recording).

↓ QR CODES

IMAGE 2.4   *QR code linking to a video clip*

QR (Quick Response) codes are the fragmented black and white squares that appear on some advertisements, magazine pages, business cards, and T-shirts. They are two dimensional barcodes that can be read by mobile devices and link to web pages or short texts.

The QR code on this page will take you to a mystery video. In order to read it, you will have to download a free app onto your smartphone or tablet computer, such as QR Reader (see Appendix 7). This app makes use of the camera lens on your device to read the code and identify the link. Online connection is necessary.

It is very simple to create your own QR codes that link to websites, Wikipedia pages, or video clips. There are many free online applications and apps that allow you to do so (see Appendix 7).

QR codes can be very useful in the classroom. If students are equipped with mobile devices and wireless internet, they can connect instantly to a specific video without the usual online distractions and/or lengthy instructions from the teacher. Importantly, teachers can generate QR codes that link to videos via Safeshare (see Appendix 7) rather than linking directly to YouTube.

QR codes are quite fun and can be integrated into a number of activities, some examples of which we will see later.

Try this ☞   **Including a QR code**

When creating a handout for students which refers to an online video (a transcript, for example), include a QR code somewhere on the page. That way, students will always be able to access the video themselves whenever they want.

Part 2

Video content for the classroom

3   Characteristics of online video

Not long ago, video in the classroom usually referred to commercially available DVDs and VHS cassettes. Video content was often linked with the world of television and cinema.

In the last few years, video has been redefined. Video-sharing culture has introduced us to new genres, new creative techniques, new aesthetics, new types of marketing, new issues, and new responsibilities. So what features of online video are most relevant to language teachers? Here are some thoughts:

User-generated content

Every minute, 72 hours of video content are uploaded onto YouTube (official 2013 figure) and most of this comes from ordinary people like you and me.

If we were looking for the quintessential user-generated video, we might choose *Charlie bit my finger*, a short family video in which a naughty baby tests his new teeth on his big brother's finger: see Video 3.1. The video was uploaded onto YouTube in 2007 and has been viewed half a billion times. It is also the perfect example of a viral video (a video that becomes popular through online sharing).

Interactivity

The consumption of online video is not a passive process. People share videos, comment on them, and blog about them. But interaction goes much deeper than that.

Virtually any viral video will be copied, remixed, and parodied. For example, there are thousands of amateur videos on YouTube that make reference to *Charlie bit my finger* in some way or another. There are *Charlie bit my finger* songs, animated versions, and reenactments. There is a trailer for a non-existent *Charlie bit my finger* horror film. There is a *Charlie bit my finger* spoof review in which a critic discusses the video as if it were a serious art film. There are hybrid videos in which *Charlie bit my finger* is remixed with other well-known viral videos.

Try this ☞ **Copies, remixes, and parodies**

Teenagers may respond well to homework assignments that involve remixing or parodying well-known viral videos. For example, students could collaborate to create their own videos in which they do any of the following:

- Make a video of a reenactment of a viral video with an English monologue or dialogue
- Create a spoof review of a viral video
- Create a spoof trailer for a sequel to a viral video
- Remix a viral video and provide a sports-style running commentary over the top
- Remix a viral video involving animals or babies and include subtitles which translate their barks, meows, or babbles into English.

Ask students to upload their work onto a video-sharing site and see whose video becomes the most popular. This can be measured in view count.

Accessibility

I remember an argument in a staffroom between two teachers. One of them had been hiding some school DVDs from his colleagues. He was making sure that they would be available whenever he needed them.

Materials no longer have to be kept out of the sight and reach of other teachers. Importantly for students, the videos that are used in class can potentially be accessed out of class. Revisiting videos in this way can be important for the purposes of revision and self-study.

Length

In the days of DVDs and VHS cassettes, teachers who used video in the classroom were often faced with a dilemma: whether to use feature films or TV episodes in their entirety, or whether to use short excerpts. The former option would mean turning the classroom into a cinema. The latter option meant that students would be denied the full story.

The internet has had a huge impact on video length. Viral videos in particular tend to be very short. *Charlie bit my finger*, for example, offers a complete story in less than a minute. As a result, length need no longer be an issue.

This is perfect for the classroom. It allows students to get the whole narrative rather than an excerpt. Completeness means better comprehension of texts. Shortness challenges us, the teachers, to design activities that aim to maximize student interaction with the material.

Stories

News stories

More stories are being caught on camera than ever before, and an increasing number of news reports are complemented by eyewitness video footage. The modern news consumer is assumed to have access to the bigger picture, and we should remember this when selecting news material for the classroom.

Try this ☞ **Engaging students with a newspaper**

Find a news article that evolves around a video – an event that was caught on camera, for example. In the classroom, play the video and ask students to speculate on the details of the story – the *where, what, when, why,* and *who,* for example. Give out copies of the text and ask students to read it to compare the facts with their predictions.

Personal stories

Of course, not all stories are newsworthy. *Charlie bit my finger* moments are quite unremarkable and happen every day. But when caught on camera and shared online, a personal story can become a local story, and a local story can go global. More and more of the narratives that enter our collective story bank originate from video-sharing culture.

Every culture has its own digital folk tales that have emerged on video-sharing sites. In multicultural groups, we can take advantage of this by asking students to share their own social media stories.

On page 112, we will see how online video narratives can be used for the basis of teacher-led storytelling sessions.

Spoken texts

The rise of online video means a rise in spoken texts. For example:

Harry: Ha ha. Charlie. Charlie bit me.
Charlie: Waah!
Harry: Ouch! Ouch! Ouch Charlie! Ouuuuuch! Charlie, that really hurt!
Charlie: He he. Ha ha!
Harry: Charlie bit me. And that really hurt Charlie, and it's still hurting.

The features of written and spoken language can differ a great deal. For example, the above text gives us a good example of the adverb *really* to emphasize a verb – a feature that is especially common in spoken English.

Video sites provide us with many different spoken text types including monologues, narrations, presentations, explanations, dialogues, verbal exchanges, and interviews. They also offer a wide range of English accents and dialects for study. Online video could potentially bring an end to the use of written texts to teach spoken language.

↓ GENRES

We are all aware of the standard genres that have evolved for DVDs. They include action, children's, classics, comedy, documentary, drama, fitness, horror, music, and television.

Online video content is particularly resistant to such classification. Despite that, we will attempt to describe a few genres of online video – especially those of interest to language teachers. This list is by no means comprehensive or complete.

Video content from yesteryear

Online video is not just about the new. The internet is an archive of 20th century footage and moving images. Most of the following have Wikipedia pages, many of which contain the videos in question:

Type of video	Example
Early moving pictures	*Roundhay Garden Scene* (1888), the oldest surviving film in existence.
Historical speeches	*I have a Dream*, a 1963 public speech by activist Martin Luther King, Jr.
Historical footage	*Happy Birthday, Mr. President*, sung by Marilyn Monroe in 1962.
Old newsreels	A 1930 newsreel in which Anne Sullivan demonstrates how she taught Helen Keller to speak.
Famous sporting moments	Jesse Owens at the 1936 Olympic Games.
Public information films and propaganda	*Duck and Cover*, a 1951 film aimed at US schoolchildren, which offered advice on how best to survive a nuclear attack.

TABLE 3.1   *Some examples of historic videos that can be seen online*

Television

Virtually any notable TV clip or highlight can find its way online, either legally or illegally (we will discuss this distinction in the next chapter). We can make use of:

- Famous TV moments
- Clips from game shows
- Clips from cookery programmes
- Comedy sketches
- Excerpts from documentaries (nature, history, science, art, etc.)
- Interviews
- News reports
- Weather reports
- Children's programmes.

Television and online video have a very close relationship. Many videos that go viral originate from television. YouTube, for example, seems to have a love for **bloopers** – unexpected mishaps that happen during live TV broadcasts.

Branded content

Many television channels, networks, production companies, studios, news agencies, and sports franchises have their own websites or branded YouTube channels. This means that a huge number of movie clips, TV highlights, sports events, etc. are legally available for teachers to use. Example channels on YouTube include *Britain's Got Talent, Sesame Street, Monty Python*, and *The Olympic Games* (see Appendix 2 for a more complete list of branded channels on YouTube).

Video memes and fads

The full story of *Charlie bit my finger* is much bigger than that told in the one-minute video. The viral video is located at the heart of a network of online interaction. There are references to it in popular culture. It has featured in news reports. It even has its own Wikipedia page. At the height of its popularity, *Charlie bit my finger* was what we would refer to as an internet meme – an interactive internet fad which spreads via digital word of mouth. Here are some more examples of video memes, most of which have their own Wikipedia pages for further exploration:

- *Free hugs campaign* (2006): Juan Mann created this video in which he offers free hugs to strangers in the street. The video went viral and generated thousands of similar videos.
- *Keyboard cat* (2007): Fatso the cat wears a blue shirt and plays an electronic keyboard. He appears at the end of tens of thousands of online videos, usually to 'play off' the main feature.
- *Rickrolling* (2008): A famous internet prank in which a seemingly relevant hyperlink would unexpectedly lead to the music video for the 1987 Rick Astley song *Never gonna give you up*.
- *Fenton!* (2011): A dog chases a herd of deer in Richmond Park, London, as his owner desperately tries to regain control. The video became the subject of hundreds of parody videos.
- *Nyan cat* (2011): Nyan is a happy cartoon cat. He flies through space, accompanied by a catchy Japanese pop song. This is a perfect example of internet bizarreness. Understanding Nyan is a key to understanding young people.
- *Harlem shake* (2013): The *Harlem shake* is probably the most interactive internet meme to date. At the height of its popularity, 4000 videos were uploaded daily. The craze started in early 2013 when five Australian teenagers created a dance format to accompany the song Harlem shake, by US DJ Baauer. The video that they uploaded inspired thousands of groups of people to create and share similar videos.

Try this ☞ **Educate the teacher**

Tell your teenage students that you are completely confused by video meme culture. Ask them to prepare presentations in which they choose a video meme case study and attempt to explain the story behind it. Ask them to:

- Describe the video which gave birth to the meme
- Investigate the story behind the video (*who*, *where*, *when*, *why*, and *how*?)
- Describe how others interacted with it.

Students could work in groups. They could choose their own video memes or you could offer suggestions (see list above).

Caught on camera

As video-recording devices proliferate and develop, they find themselves in the hands of more and more people. They also find themselves in some new and unexpected places: on car dashboards; on the helmets of extreme sportspeople; attached to wild or domestic animals; on remote control helicopters; inside the International Space Station.

As a result, more and more incidents, accidents, mishaps (often called 'fail' videos), crimes, cute babies, and animal antics are caught on camera, and shared online by amateurs. This is the comedy and tragedy of online video.

The following videos can be seen by typing the title into a video search engine (see Appendix 7).

- *Very large hail*: Hailstones the size of golfballs! An example of extreme weather caught on camera.
- *Why it's good to have a dash camera*: A conman and woman are exposed as they try to scam a motorist by reversing into him.
- *Battle at Kruger*: Filmed at a national park in South Africa, this amateur video captured a confrontation between a herd of buffalo, a pride of lions, and some crocodiles.
- *Crab bites nose*: Soldier antagonizes crab. Crab grabs nose with claw and pinches hard. Contains swearing (in Russian).
- *Cat gets caught barking by a human and resumes meowing*: The title says it all.
- *Bizkit the sleep-walking dog*: A dog lying on his side starts to run in his sleep. He gets up and runs into a wall. Very funny.
- *Ice cream thief* (*Dozde Bastani* in Persian): A father comes downstairs early one morning and catches his little boy stealing ice-cream from the fridge.

Advertising

Online, the absolute goal of any advertiser is to create a situation in which users interact, positively, with a campaign. The idea is to generate a popular culture around the brand or product.

Sometimes this happens by accident. For example, on video-sharing sites, Lego and Post-it notes are very popular with amateur film enthusiasts who use them to create stop-motion animations. This has generated free publicity for the brands (see Video 3.2 for example).

Usually, however, advertisers have to work to capture the minds of the public. As a result, viral marketing campaigns are becoming increasingly clever and imaginative. As integral parts of online campaigns, adverts on video sites must be intriguing, appealing, interesting, moving, or fun. Brands that have achieved this include the following:

- Cadbury's ('Gorilla' campaign)
- Old Spice ('The Man Your Man Could Smell Like' campaign)
- Blendtec ('Will it Blend?' campaign)
- Evian ('Roller Babies' campaign)
- T-Mobile ('Dance' campaign)
- Dove ('Dove Evolution' and 'Real Sketches' campaigns).

The *Dove Real Beauty Sketches* campaign (see Video 3.3), made use of a short film in which a forensic artist sketches a number of women according to descriptions of them. The aim was to demonstrate that women are more beautiful than they think. A video like this has a powerful narrative which can be used in the language classroom. It will also generate a lot of interest and teachers can look for texts (articles, blog posts, etc.) which report on the campaign and explore issues that it raises. For example, is the message behind the advert a positive one? Or does it have an underlying and unintended implication that beauty is still what defines women?

Try this ☞ **Viral marketing campaign**

Ask students to write about a viral marketing campaign that involves online video. There are always many to choose from. Ask them to describe the online advert(s), identify what is original about the campaign, and explain how it attempts to encourage online interaction.

Ambiguity

One way to intrigue an audience is to use ambiguity. Online, it is often not clear whether a video is an advert or not. *Guy has glasses tattooed on his face*, is one example. As the title suggests, it makes for uncomfortable viewing. It looks like an amateur video. But is it real? And if not, who is trying to fool us and why?

The answer is that the video is an advert for Ray-Ban sunglasses. In the classroom, **stealth adverts** like this can be engaging and thought-provoking. Other examples include *Kobe Bryant jumps over a speeding car* (Nike) and *Guys backflip into jeans* (Levis).

Try this ☞ **Is it real?**

The authenticity of many viral videos is questionable. When using such videos in the classroom, there are three key questions that can be put to students for speculative discussion or online research:

- Authenticity: Is the video real?
- Creators: Who is behind the video?
- Motives: Why was it created?

Other types of adverts that teachers can make use of include:

- Social awareness adverts and campaigns
- Political campaigns
- Low-budget adverts for local businesses that go viral (often for ironic reasons)
- Trailers for films, books, and computer games
- Parodies of bad infomercials which, in turn, result in increased publicity for the product.

Short films and art projects

Other online video adverts

The democratization of video tools has led to an explosion of online creativity. Video sites are packed with short films, video art, and animations. Here are a few examples which can easily be found by entering the title into a video search engine (see Appendix 7).

- *The Black hole*: A sinister short film in which a man discovers a small portable black hole and then gets greedy. Created by Phil Sansom and Olly Williams, the film is part of the Future Shorts label.
- *Marcel the shell with shoes on*: A stop-motion animated short film about an anthropomorphic shell. A collaboration between Jenny Slate and Dean Fleischer-Camp.
- *Breakfast: Fortified with iron*: A group of young men prepare bacon, eggs, and toast with an iron (i.e. the type used for pressing clothes). Directed by Tom Scott.
- *Rubber bands vs. water melon*: Gavin Free and Daniel Gruchy – better known as The Slow Mo Guys – create beautiful slow motion photography of a watermelon that explodes when 500 rubber bands are wrapped around it.
- *MUTO: a wall-painted animation*: Created by BLU, a street artist who creates short films of animated graffiti.
- *Western spaghetti*: Created by director PES, who uses everyday objects to make stop-motion animation. Other films include *Human skateboard*, *Fresh guacamole*, and *KaBoom*!
- *Noah takes a photo of himself every day for six years:* One of the first passage of time projects that led to many others.
- *I met the walrus*: In 1969, a 14-year-old boy named Jerry Levitan sneaked into John Lennon's Toronto hotel room with a tape recorder. In this video, directed by Josh Raskin, the interview has been animated.
- *Forgetfulness*: A poem read by its author Billy Collins and illustrated by Julian Grey.

Music

Radio plays used to be the way for bands and singers to get exposure. These days it often requires a viral video.

One of the first groups to discover the power of online video was *OK GO!* In their most famous video, *Here it goes again*, the group members perform an intricately-choreographed series of dance moves across two rows of treadmills.

More recently, in 2012, the world was taken over by South Korean Psy's *Gangnam Style*, the first online video to reach over one billion views.

User-generated musical content

Some of the most interesting online music videos and cultures are user generated. Here are a few examples:

- **Musical remixes of viral videos:** Popular viral videos often find themselves being remixed as songs. To see an example of this, type *Charlie bit my finger song* into a video search engine (see Appendix 7). Perhaps the best known creators of such videos are the Gregory Brothers. An example of their work can be seen at:
  – Original version: Video 3.4.
  – Song version: Video 3.5.

- **Lip dubs:** in a lip dub video, individuals film themselves lip synching to a song and then dub the song into their video at the editing stage. There are tens of thousands of lip dub videos online, many of which are the result of teacher–student or even whole-school collaborations (type 'lip dub school' into a video search engine). Lip dub videos generally require a lot of preparation: they are usually filmed in a single unedited shot in which the camera person follows the 'singers' through rooms, corridors, the playground, etc.
- **Literal version music videos:** The original literal version music video was a parody of *Take on me* by 1980s Norwegian pop group, *A-ha*. The literal version is the same as the official version, except that the actual lyrics are replaced by bogus lyrics that comically describe the visuals in the video.
- **Misheard lyrics videos:** Similar to literal version music videos are misheard lyric versions. These often consist of the original music video with accompanying subtitles to show the misheard lyrics. In one example, the lyrics to Eric Carmen's 1975 hit *All by myself, don't wanna be all by myself any more* are represented as: *Obama's elf, don't wanna be Obama's elf any more*. Sometimes, visuals are replaced with new ones to reflect the misheard lyrics in some way or another.
- **Unofficial fan videos:** These are often uploaded onto sites like YouTube where they compete for popularity alongside the official versions. A good example is the unofficial video for *Kids*, by US band *MGMT*. (Video 3.6). It was created as part of a project assignment by film student Jon Salmon. His video featured two of his fellow students dancing and miming the lyrics to the song. To date, his video has been viewed over fifty million times – almost four times as many as the band's own official video. Another example is the video for *Shop Vac* (Video 3.7), a song by singer Jonathan Coulton, who actively encourages fans to interact with his work. The video makes use of an animation technique called 'kinetic typography' which is the technical name for moving text. The song lyrics appear on screen as they are sung. They move around in a variety of arrays and typefaces and are accompanied by graphics which drive the narrative of the song.

Try this ☞ **Imagining a music video**

Having multiple videos for popular songs allows for tasks in which students compare interpretations and narratives. Play a song (audio only) to students and give them a copy of the lyrics. Put them into groups and tell them that they are teams of film producers. Their task is to conceive a video to accompany the song. Each group produces a written brief of the video that they envisage. Let groups present their ideas to each other and decide which is the best one. Finally, show students the actual music videos that accompany the song (both official and unofficial) and let them decide which one they like the best.

Try this ☞ **Finding kinetic typography videos**

Kinetic typography videos (such as the unofficial fan video described above) can be engaging in the language classroom, and there are many online. The technique is often used to provide a visual element to audio texts such as presentations, telephone calls, radio broadcasts, interviews, poems, and famous film scenes (not just songs). Try typing the words 'Kinetic typography' into a video search engine (see Appendix 7).

Presentations

Many channels of communication, which are traditionally associated with the written word, are being replaced or complemented by video. Journalists, critics, educators, PR people, scientists, job applicants, and even students either choose, or are required, to communicate ideas in front of cameras. It is also becoming the norm for conference talks to be filmed and shared online. In many sectors, good presenting skills are more important than ever before.

There are many online videos in which presenters from a wide range of academic, scientific, artistic, philosophical, and religious backgrounds communicate ideas and share stories. Two very good sources are TED and Big Think (see Appendix 1). Both of these sites include transcripts and translations of the presenters' words. Some example presentations are listed below.

- *Is education killing creativity?* (Ken Robinson on TED.com)
- *The danger of a single story* (Chimamanda Adichie on TED.com)
- *Don't insist on English!* (Patricia Ryan on TED.com)
- *The world's English mania* (Jay Walker on TED.com)
- *How not to spend your whole day on Facebook* (Charles Duhigg on BigThink.com)
- *Morality without religion* (Franz de Waal on Big Think.com).

Try this ☞ **Evaluate a presenter**

Choose a good presentation and ask students to evaluate the presenter by focusing on non-verbal aspects of his or her performance. Ask students to make notes about any of the following: eyes and eye contact; gestures; facial expressions; hands; arms; body position; pace of speech; intonation: use of silence; posture; clothing.

Try this ☞ **Present a presentation**

For a homework task, ask students to find an online presentation that interests them. Ask them to summarize the presenter's message so that it can be communicated in one minute. Later, students can present their summaries to the rest of the class. Alternatively, they can create videos of their own in which they speak about their chosen presentations.

Instructional and demonstration videos

Video-sharing culture has made it possible for millions of enthusiastic individuals to share their everyday expertise with the world. Through informal instructional videos on sites like YouTube, we can learn, for example:

- How to moonwalk like Michael Jackson
- How to make the perfect cup of tea
- How to make an origami animal
- How to peel a banana like a monkey
- How to get an egg in a milk bottle
- How to throw a boomerang and catch it
- How to make a stop-motion animation with Lego
- How to frame a shot with a video camera

- How to photograph a flying cat
- How to survive a zombie attack.

There are a number of video sites dedicated to such videos. Videojug, for example (Appendix 1), provides videos to cover a range of categories such as food and drink, love and relationships, money and careers, and health and fitness.

Try this ☞ **Everyone an expert**

Introduce students to the idea that everyone is an expert at something, regardless of how trivial or valuable that thing is. Show students two or three online instructional videos and draw attention to any key language used by the instructors. For homework, ask students to create videos of their own to demonstrate their chosen skills.

Science videos

Thanks to online video, the lives of teachers who are required to teach science through English are easier and safer. Videos of experiments and demonstrations, which could not be performed in the classroom for reasons of practicality or safety, can be found online. All of the following questions can be answered by videos on YouTube:

- What happens when you drop a hammer and a feather from the same height on the moon? Which one will hit the ground first?
- What happens when you inhale sulphur dioxide?
- What happens when you throw a pan of boiling water into –40° Siberian air?
- What happens when you scare a possum?
- What happens when you put a Mentos (a small chewy mint) into a bottle of Diet Coke?
- What happens when you put marshmallows into a vacuum?
- What happens when a supersonic plane reaches 1,234 kilometres per hour?

Try this ☞ **Zero conditional science quiz**

Find a number of clips which demonstrate principles such as the ones mentioned above. Create a quiz for your learners and ask them to attempt to answer the 'What happens when ...?' questions. Later, play the videos and find out who came closest to the correct answers. Alternatively, create a QR code for each video (see page 40), put them around the classroom walls and allow students to access the videos on mobile devices.

Video bloggers

Video bloggers (or vloggers) tend to be young, dedicated, and savvy. In regularly-uploaded videos, they address the camera and share their thoughts, views, opinions, and stories. Established video bloggers can generate huge online followings.

At worst, video bloggers can be narcissistic and banal. At best, however, they can be interesting, entertaining, or moving. The following video bloggers can be seen on YouTube:

- Charlie McDonnell: The first YouTuber in the UK to reach one million subscribers, Charlie is young, English, and instantly likeable. His videos deal with existential matters as well as science and tea.
- Lex Croucher: Lex is a young British graduate in English literature who started video blogging while at university. She is strong, opinionated, irreverent, and popular with teenage girls.
- Ze Frank: A pioneer of the video blogging format, Ze Frank has used his videos to create communities and persuade followers (successfully) to take on challenges such as create an 'Earth sandwich' where individuals were asked to collaborate to simultaneously place two pieces of bread perfectly opposite each other on our planet.
- Chris Hadfield: The 'internet's favourite astronaut'. Chris Hadfield video blogged from the International Space Station before he retired.
- Hendrik Ball: An eccentric English gentleman who demonstrates his collection of unusual antique toys.

Talent

YouTube is the biggest stage for talent the world has ever seen. The beautiful thing is that some talents and skills that would otherwise have been unheard of, have come into the limelight. All of the following can be seen on YouTube:

- *Balancing 15 books on my head while reciting pi to the 100th digit and solving a Rubik's cube* (type it into YouTube).
- *21 Accents*: Actress Amy Walker brilliantly demonstrates her accent impersonation skills.
- *One pound fish*: A trader at a London market demonstrates the song he sings to sell fish. A nice song to use with English beginners.

Pranks, stunts, and practical jokes

Finally, what human pastime could be more natural than doing something funny or dangerous, filming it, and sharing the result online? On video-sharing sites, this practice is taken to an art form. Here are some examples of videos that can be found using a video search engine (see Appendix 7):

- *Guys skis down tube escalator*: The escalator in question is located at Angel Station in the London Underground. It is supposedly the longest escalator in Europe.
- *Frozen Grand Central*: A large group of people simultaneously freeze for five minutes in Grand Central Station, New York. The stunt was organized by the performance art group Improv Everywhere.
- *JK wedding entrance dance*: A popular wedding viral video. The ushers, the groomsmen, the bridesmaids, the groom, and finally the bride enter the church and dance down the aisle.
- *Dead student – prank on teacher*: Some naughty Norwegian schoolboys get a classmate to lie on the classroom floor and then cover him with fake blood. Then the teacher walks in. A reason not to put video cameras in the hands of students.

- *Honiton Community College teachers*: This video consists of a collage of interviews with final year students at a school. However, unknown to each interviewee, a gang of dancing teachers has hijacked the background of their video.
- *Amazing water trick! How to suspend water without a cup!* YouTube user Dan DeEntremont demonstrates a way of lifting an inverted glass of water off the table to leave a beautifully suspended column of water. However, it is not real – Dan has used computer animated graphics.

4   Finding and selecting videos

Knowing how to discover new video content can require skill. And ensuring that it is suitable for your students requires some thought. This chapter looks at ways to find videos for your classroom as well as issues to consider.

↓ FINDING VIDEOS

Video searches

Whether you are looking for a specific video that you have seen before, or a generic video to complement a classroom activity, you will need to identify key words that are associated with the video (*baby + panda + sneeze*, for example) and use these for the basis of an online search.

Finding the right search terms often requires lateral thinking. For example, if you want to find a video of a TV weather report to use in class, you might be disappointed when a search of the words *weather + report* results in many clips of the 1970s jazz fusion band *Weather Report* in concert. In this case, try running a new search but use the terms *weather + forecast* instead.

There are three principle places to carry out video searches:

1 Standard search engines

If you already know the title of a video that you are looking for, the simplest way to find it can be through a standard search engine. For example, type the words *Charlie bit my finger* into Yahoo, Google, or Bing, and it will bring up a thumbnail image which links directly to the video on YouTube.

2 Video sites

An alternative is to go directly to a video site such as Vimeo, YouTube, TED, or Daily Motion, and search for videos there. One big advantage of this is that video sites usually offer search options which make it easier to find what you want. For example, Vimeo allows you to specify the maximum length of the video that you are looking for. TED allows you to search for videos which have subtitles in your language. YouTube allows you to select videos according to popularity. On most sites, you will find these functions in the advanced search options. It is worth becoming familiar with the search options for the video sites that you use the most.

Try this ☞   **Narrowing a specific search**

If you are looking for a video that you have seen before, make use of advanced search options to narrow your search. For example, if you are looking for the sneezing baby panda video on YouTube, filter your search results to include only short videos.

Try this ☞   **Generic searches**

If your video site has an advanced search option that allows you to order your search results by popularity, it can be useful when making generic searches. The principle is that the most popular videos may be the ones that are most worth watching, although this isn't always the case. For example, by typing the words *weather + forecast*, into YouTube and filtering results by popularity, you may find the following videos:

- The funniest weather forecast bloopers
- A clip from the BBC in which Prince Charles was invited to present the weather forecast at the end of the news
- A clip in which a meteorologist shows us behind the scenes of a television weather forecast.

3 Video search engines

There are a number of video search engines and apps such as Google Video and Bing Videos (see Appendix 7). Note that these are not video-hosting sites. They allow us to conduct searches for videos across the entire web. Sometimes, however, they can be quite biased in their search results. For example, the results of Google Video searches tend to include a particularly high proportion of videos that are hosted on YouTube (YouTube is owned by Google).

Try this ☞   **Excluding YouTube from a video search**

Type any search term or phrase into Google Video and follow it with −YouTube (i.e. the minus sign directly followed by YouTube). By doing this, the results of your search will not include any videos from YouTube.

Discovering videos

Discovering good videos can be like discovering good music. You have to know which venues to visit, which magazines to read, which radio stations to listen to, which people to talk to, and which record shops to frequent. Here are some ideas for letting the good material come directly to you.

Awareness

There is often no need to discover online videos for yourself. They will often come directly via everyday sources like online newspapers, teenagers, or social media sites. Whenever you find yourself watching an engaging online video, consider that it might be suitable for teaching purposes. In Part 3, we will look at lesson planning ideas.

Subscriptions

One of the best ways to discover new videos is to take advantage of subscription possibilities on video sites. For example, you might like the short films that are uploaded onto YouTube by the Future Shorts film label. If so, visit the Future Shorts channel on YouTube and click on subscribe. You can choose to be notified of new Future Shorts videos by email every time a new one is uploaded.

Discovery sites

There are a number of websites, apps, and online communities that can be useful for discovering online video. Examples include Reddit and StumbleUpon (see Appendix 7 for more information).

↓ SUITABILITY OF MATERIAL

Television content is screened, structured, and scheduled. In the United Kingdom, for example, you might sit down at seven o'clock to watch the news. Then, you'll expect a programme suitable for the family. At nine o'clock, it's time for the children to go to bed. Until then, nothing shown would be unsuitable for young eyes. You know where you are with TV.

Online video isn't like that. You may decide to watch a video based on its title and thumbnail image alone. Or you may arrive at a video through a hypertext link. In such cases, you may have little or no idea what is going to come out of the video window on your computer screen.

When you leave behind the safety of the coursebook, you face many potential hazards. When you bring online video into the classroom, you are dealing with a medium that requires special caution. Although popular video sites set rules about what type of content can and cannot be uploaded, a lot of videos containing sexually explicit content, hate (racism, sexism, etc.), abuse, humiliation, bullying, and violence will evade the filters.

Moving images can be particularly shocking. I remember once seeing a fatal rock climbing accident on YouTube without being prepared for how much the horror of it would affect me. And although only a very naive teacher would willingly show such a video in class, things sometimes don't go according to plan. For example:

- A video that you thought would work well in class turns out to be mildly offensive for a number of students.
- After playing a video on a popular video-sharing site a student persuades you to click on one of the suggested videos. It turns out to be quite unsuitable.
- After playing a video on a popular video-sharing site, you are presented with a number of thumbnail images for suggested videos, some of which appear quite sexually explicit.

Here are some guidelines for caution:

1 If you are unsure about the suitability of a video for your students, ask a colleague for advice. Even better, put your question to a group of

colleagues, and look for a consensus. The staffroom is the perfect place for support of this kind.

2   Avoid playing in class videos that you have not seen before.

3   Vet your videos well: before using one in class, make sure that you have watched it in its entirety. You do not want any unexpected surprises.

4   Avoid playing videos in class directly on popular video sites. Download them if legal. If not, use a site such as Safeshare (see Appendix 7) to block out suggestions for other videos, as well as adverts and comments.

5   If you have to look for a video on YouTube in class, make sure that the safety mode is on (see Appendix 4). This will avoid videos that contain inappropriate content, although it is not completely reliable.

↓ INVESTIGATING A VIDEO

There are many reasons why you may feel the need to investigate a video. You may want to know, for example:

• Who uploaded it
• When it was uploaded
• Whether or not it was uploaded by its rightful owner
• Whether it is real or if it involves trickery
• How to get in touch with the person who uploaded it.

Let's take an example. In the previous chapter, we referred to a mysterious video in which a young man has a pair of sunglasses tattooed on his face (see page 50). If you go to YouTube and run a search of 'glasses tattooed', you will see that multiple copies of the video have been uploaded onto the site. This is very common for viral videos. It usually results from unimaginative users cloning the video and uploading it on their own channels in an attempt to benefit from the video's popularity.

Uploader

How can you establish which is the legitimate version? In many cases, we only have to look for a recognizable brand – the name of the individual or group that uploaded the video (BBCEarth, Monty Python, TED talks Director, PES film, etc.) In the case of the tattooed sunglasses videos, this is not an option, so we have to use other means.

Date of upload

Many video sites such as YouTube show the exact dates on which videos are uploaded. This can be useful for finding the legitimate version of a video, since it will usually be the first one to be uploaded onto the site.

View count

Another important clue is view count. The legitimate video will usually be the one that has most views. In the case of the tattooed sunglasses, one version has been viewed over two million times. The other versions come nowhere close to this.

Other work

Having decided that the video uploaded by *neverhidefilms* is the legitimate one, we can click on it and explore further. By clicking on the name of the individual or group that uploaded the video (in this case *neverhidefilms*), we can visit their account (or channel) and see what other videos they have uploaded.

In the case of *neverhidefilms*, we discover that the group has uploaded a number of other videos, all of which involve sunglasses, and many of which involve similar ambiguity. An internet search of *neverhidefilms* tells us that it is the official YouTube channel for Ray-Ban sunglasses. It is safe to assume that *Guy has glasses tattooed on his face* is an advert.

Other information

By visiting a user's channel or account, it is possible to get additional information such as user profiles, biodata, and contact information.

↓ COPYRIGHT

In the last decade, the distinction between content creator and content consumer has blurred. Online, creativity feeds creativity. Users get involved and interact with each other's content in ways that were impossible before the internet existed.

Out of this culture, questions that previously didn't concern us need to be asked. When can we use other people's content? And what are we allowed to do with it? What is legal and what is not? Taking YouTube as a case study, let's look at issues of copyright which concern everyone.

Uploading content on YouTube

In its community guidelines, YouTube states that you should:

Respect copyright. Only upload videos that you made or that you are authorized to use. This means don't upload videos that you didn't make, or use content in your videos which someone else owns the copyright to, such as music tracks, snippets of copyrighted programs, or videos made by other users, without necessary authorizations.

Despite this, there are still many examples of copyright violations on the site. Many of the video clips that originate from television – comedy sketches, news reports, excerpts from nature documentaries, etc. would fall into this category. Much of this illegally-uploaded material goes unnoticed.

Sometimes, users upload whole films or entire TV series onto YouTube, accompanied by naive disclaimers which say something along the lines of: *Disclaimer: I do not own this content. I have uploaded it for entertainment purposes only. No copyright violation intended.*

The Content ID programme

Content owners who wish to protect their creative property may register with YouTube's Content ID programme. This allows their copyrighted material to be identified when it is uploaded onto YouTube without consent. In such situations, the content owner has two main options:

1 Request that the video is blocked and removed from YouTube.

2 Allow the video to remain on YouTube, but allow YouTube to include adverts beside it. In this way, the video is monetized, and YouTube shares revenue with the content owner.

In a 2010 TED talk, Margaret Stewart, YouTube's head of user experience claimed that, 'Most rights owners, instead of blocking, will allow the copy to be published and then they benefit through the exposure, advertising, and linked sales.' She argued that, 'By simply blocking all reuse, you'll miss out on new art forms, new audiences, new distribution channels, and new revenue streams.'

Stewart is not referring to full-length, byte-by-byte, verbatim copies of videos, films, or TV episodes. She is referring to videos that are creatively changed or adapted in some way, so that new meaning is created. She could be talking about either of the two unofficial fan videos that were referred to in the previous chapter. In the case of the *MGMT* song *Kids* (see page 52), Sony Music Entertainment decided not to remove the fan video from YouTube, but to benefit from the publicity and revenue that it generated.

Creative Commons

There is currently a lot of discussion and debate about whether or not individuals should be legally permitted to edit and combine existing materials. On one hand, there is a philosophical argument that a remix culture is a desirable one. On the other hand, protective content owners stand by copyright laws to prevent it.

Out of this debate, an international non-profit organization called Creative Commons has emerged. Creative Commons is dedicated to expanding the pool of creative works that are legally available for others to copy, transform, and combine. The last few years have seen more and more musicians, filmmakers, writers, bloggers, photographers, and other creators publish their work with Creative Commons licences.

Singer-songwriter Jonathan Coulton, mentioned in Chapter 3, is an example of an artist who publishes his work under such a licence. The specific licence that he has chosen allows anyone to use and adapt his songs in any way they like, as long as:

● His work is attributed
● It is used for non-commercial purposes.

It was because of this licence that one fan was able to create the unofficial, kinetic typography music video for his song *Shop Vac* without permission and without problems (see page 52). The use of a Creative Commons licence may have contributed to Jonathan Coulton's success.

A lot of videos on YouTube as well as other sites such as Vimeo, Wikimedia Commons, and TED (see Appendix 1) are uploaded with a Creative Commons licence. Such videos can usually be found using the advanced search options that were discussed on page 58. Note, however, that there are different types of licence and you should check specifically what the licence allows you to do with the video.

As well as video, there are many online sources of music, sound effects, and images that carry Creative Commons licences (see Appendix 6). YouTube itself has a feature called Audioswap, which allows users to select Creative Commons music to accompany their own video work.

Copyright questions

Here are a number of questions that I am frequently asked by teachers.

Do I have to get permission to use a video in class?

For any legitimate video on YouTube, there is no need to obtain permission to play it in class.

Do I have to get permission to embed a video on a website?

When uploading a video onto YouTube, the user can specify whether or not it can be embedded. In other words, if the user does not want you to embed a video, they can easily prevent this from happening.

How do I find out if a YouTube video has been uploaded legally or not?

If you are in doubt, and as a general guiding rule, if a video clip is accompanied by adverts, then it has either been uploaded by the rightful owner, or claimed by the rightful owner through the Copyright ID programme. Adverts can be shown onscreen before the video starts, they can pop up on the screen while the video plays or they can be included beside the video window. In the case of music videos, film clips, and excerpts from TV series, viewers may also be invited to buy the content via a link to an online store.

Is it acceptable to use a clip that has been uploaded illegally?

If a clip has been uploaded onto YouTube without the owner's consent, and if it has not been claimed through the Content ID programme, you should not use it in class. In addition there is a practical problem: the video may be suddenly removed from YouTube without warning.

Is it legal to download videos from YouTube?

There are many online applications, browser plugins, and mobile apps that allow users to download or 'capture' online videos from video sites (see Appendix 7). For YouTube, however, doing so is a violation of the site's Terms of Use. That means that it can be possible to download a video from YouTube without breaking any copyright laws – if the video has a Creative Commons licence, for example. But it is impossible to do so without breaking YouTube's own guidelines.

5   Creating your own content

A teacher friend of mine often used to invite his father into his classroom to speak to his adult learners. They were always fascinated with the stories that he shared – many of them involving his own son in some way or other.

Human beings are fascinated by other human beings. Bringing a family member into your classroom can be a memorable, language-rich experience. Unfortunately, it can also be impractical, inappropriate, or against school regulations. A video can be the next best thing.

Take Rollo, for example. As a good friend of mine, I have referred to him in class on a number of occasions.

My students have always been intrigued about Rollo because of his name. In Spanish, the word *rollo* has a number of meanings, all of which sound quite strange for a man's name. For a while, they even refused to believe that he existed. It seemed natural, then, to introduce Rollo to my students through a short video and ask him to say hello (Video 5.1).

With just a little planning and preparation, a simple video-recording device allows a teacher to capture personalized spoken texts from English-speaking friends, family members, colleagues, and acquaintances. The resulting videos can be used for a variety of teaching purposes. For example, they can be used to study language, give deeper meaning to a coursebook topic, or provide sample spoken texts on which students can model their own (more about this in Chapter 8).

↓ CONSIDERATIONS

Finding volunteers

Regardless of where you are in the world, you will always have access to expert users of English. Don't assume that the people who you film must be native speakers. Individuals who share the same cultural and linguistic backgrounds with your learners often provide the best language models.

In your search for willing subjects, consider any of the following:

- People who express themselves well
- People whose jobs require good communication (teachers, doctors, managers, anyone with presenting experience)
- Good storytellers
- People that your students already know (colleagues in your school, for example)

Creating your own content

- People that your students know of, but have never met
- Children (it can be interesting and engaging for English learners to hear how children communicate in the language. Parental permission must be obtained)
- Young people, who are often particularly comfortable in front of a camera (parental permission must be obtained)
- People with unusual accents or dialects (this is useful for studying diversity in English).

 **Getting it right**

Personal and cultural attitudes to being filmed

Be sensitive to people's feeling about being filmed. Some people hate the very idea of it and shouldn't be forced. Also be sensitive to cultural implications. For example, in many countries there are sensitivities about what should or should not be filmed.

 **Getting it right**

Uploading videos

You may want to upload a video so that students can access it in their own time, for study or revision, for example. If this is the case, you must make sure that your subject is willing and aware of your intentions. Look into privacy options that your chosen video-sharing site offers (these were discussed in Chapter 2).

Semi-scripting

It is important to have a basic idea of what you are going to say in front of a camera before the record button is pressed. Negotiate the basic outline of a monologue or the structure of an answer to a question, for example.

Encourage your subjects to grade their language to your learners. For example, suggest that they avoid low-frequency, obscure, or cultural language items if possible. Run through what they are going to say before filming. Allow subjects to make use of notes if they want but insist on heads up communication with the camera.

Note that it may require more than one attempt or 'take' to get a good result.

Framing

Plan the **framing** and composition of your shot – fill the rectangular video frame with your subject's head and shoulders. Use the rule of thirds to ensure that your subject's eyes are two thirds of the way up the screen (see figure 5.1a opposite). If your subject likes to communicate using prominent hand or arm gestures, try to keep them in the frame as well.

Don't stand too far away from your subject (see figure 5.1b). Apart from making your subject appear too small, a distance between the subject and the camera can result in unclear audio.

If you are using a mobile phone, make sure that you hold the device the correct way when filming. You don't want a vertical video (see figure 5.1c).

5.1a   5.1b   5.1c

FIGURE 5.1   *Examples of correct and incorrect framing*

Once you have composed your frame, keep it. Don't pan the camera around unnecessarily. Put it on a tripod if possible.

Choosing locations

It is annoying to have an otherwise good video ruined by a noisy background. Choose your location well. Look for quiet places away from traffic, wind, and noisy children. Also consider how your location could contribute to the meaning of the video. For example, if your subject is going to talk about food, and you are filming at home, then it would make sense to film in the kitchen or at the dining room table.

Video chat applications

Rather than filming an individual in person, you can make use of popular video chat applications such as Skype and Facetime (see Appendix 7). In order to capture an online video conversation, screencast software will be necessary (see page 40).

↓ MONOLOGUES

In the language classroom, stories are best told by human beings. Persuade camera-confident friends to share their anecdotes, memorable experiences, and jokes with your students. Such spoken texts can be invaluable for language learning. Video 5.2 is an example from Jamie Zhang from China. After telling me about an amusing misunderstanding involving her English teacher, I asked if she would mind repeating it in front of the camera.

Me: So tell me about your misunderstanding.

Jamie: All right – that was back to the year 2000 when I was studying at Leicester University and in my spare time I chose writing and pronunciation as my – you know – subject. And one day I went out with my teacher – my pronunciation teacher who is about two meters tall and I looked up at him and said wow, erm, you know – Chinese are short and he turned to me and asked me, who _____ them?

Try this ☞ **Reading**

As the above transcript demonstrates, video texts can be transcribed and used for activities that involve intensive reading. In this case, the students' task is to guess what the missing word is. They are given the clue that the misunderstanding resulted from the fact that Chinese speakers of English sometimes have problems pronouncing /r/ sounds.

Try this ☞ **Transcribing**

If you feel that a short story or monologue contains some useful language for your students, ask them to transcribe it for homework. In order for this to be possible, you will probably want to upload it onto a video-sharing site and make it accessible to students.

Try this ☞ **Comparing language**

Create videos in which different individuals tell the same story, independently from each other. For example:

- Ask a couple to tell the story of how they met (one at a time)
- Show two people a written joke. Then ask them to tell it to the camera in their own words
- Show two people a short video clip and then ask them to describe what happened. For example, Video 5.3 and Video 5.4 show two people telling the same story.

In class, ask students to compare the different ways of communicating similar ideas. This can be good for strengthening awareness of individuals and their personal language choices and perceptions of events.

Try this ☞ **Modelling a speaking task**

Look for monologue speaking tasks and activities in your coursebook in which students have to, for example:

- Recount a time in which they were misunderstood when speaking English
- Describe their daily routines
- Talk about the most courageous thing they have ever done
- Give advice to their younger self
- Describe their home.

Before class, find a friend who would be willing to engage in such an activity. Film their response, and bring the video into the classroom to introduce the task, demonstrate key language, and provide a model for students' own answers.

Try this ☞ **Speaking exam preparation**

Many speaking exams have a part in which candidates are required to talk, at length, on a subject of the examiner's choice. To prepare students for this part of the exam, make use of a past paper, an expert user of English (another teacher, for example), and a video camera. Film a good performance of a model monologue and use the video to draw students' attention to good language, good structure, and good strategies.

↓ DIALOGUES

The dynamics of spoken language change considerably when more than one person is involved. In a conversation, for example, speakers interact with each other and construct meaning cooperatively.

In Video 5.5, James and Jess share their personal feelings and thoughts about a hypothetical situation that I have put to them. In doing so, they respond to each other's ideas by questioning them, challenging them, or elaborating on them. Interestingly, without being asked to do so, they reach a consensus.

In Chapter 8 we will be examining this video in greater depth.

✓ *Getting it right*

Encouraging interaction between subjects

In the above video, I pressed the record button on the video camera, asked my question and then walked away. (In fact you can briefly see me in the background at 0:11.) It is important to create distance between yourself and your subjects in this way or you risk becoming involved in the discussion. Even if you stay silent, it is often too tempting for your subjects to look to you for reassurance and try to draw you into the conversation.

Try this ☞

Modelling or setting up a speaking activity

For any communicative speaking activity that you intend to set up in class, consider that you could create a video in which it is demonstrated by two expert users of English. Draw students' attention to any useful language that is used, and then ask them to get into pairs to construct answers of their own. The above video was created to model a 'would you rather' discussion in which students were required to make use of hypothetical 'would', and consider similar questions such as:

- Would you rather be the world's best singer or the world's best dancer?
- Would you rather time-travel to the past or the future?
- Would you rather speak English like a native or twelve other languages at elementary level?
- Would you rather be able to fly or make yourself invisible?
- Would you rather eat a sheep's eyeball or walk to work naked?

Try this ☞

Guess the relationship

Show students a video in which two people you know are conversing. Ask students to guess the relationship between them. This can add an extra depth to students' engagement with the video, the body language of the subjects, and the language that they use. You could give students a multiple choice such as:

- They are colleagues
- They have just met for the first time
- They are brother and sister (siblings)
- They are married
- They are just good friends
- They are boyfriend and girlfriend.

Try this ☞ **Turn taking**

Use a video text such as the one above to examine how interlocutors interact and cooperate. For example, transcribe the spoken text and print it off. Cut up the individual turns and ask students to attempt to put them into order. Draw attention to the way that meaning is constructed collaboratively. Finally, ask students to make a note of any language items or chunks that they would like to make their own.

Try this ☞ **Discussing a photograph**

Choose a thought-provoking photograph and select two volunteers to go in front of the camera. Start filming and hand them the photograph. Ask them if they have ever seen it before and if so, what they know about it. Give them enough space to allow them to share ideas and construct a narrative. In class, use the video to study language used to speculate about photographs (modal language, *looks like*, *looks as if*, etc.)

Try this ☞ **Discussing a video**

As above, select two volunteers to go in front of the camera. Show them a short video and then ask them to do any of the following:

- Offer an interpretation of the video
- Reconstruct the narrative
- Decide whether or not the video is real or if it involves trickery
- Decide how the video was made.

In class, use the spoken text to equip students with the language necessary for talking about videos.

Try this ☞ **Speaking exam preparation**

Many speaking exams have a section in which candidates have to converse together. Look for a past paper and find two expert English-speaking friends who would be willing to perform the task in front of a video camera. Use the video to provide a model of what is required of them. Draw students' attention to the dynamics and language of turn taking and interaction.

↓ INTERVIEWS

In Chapter 12, we will see a Try this idea, in which video chat applications (Skype, Facetime, etc.) can be used to bring individuals into our classrooms to be interviewed by students in real time (i.e. **synchronously**).

We can also use video recording tools to conduct interviews **asynchronously**, although this can require more work on the teacher's part.

Try this ☞ **Asynchronous video interview**

1 Use a video-recording device to interview a friend or acquaintance with an interesting job, hobby, or lifestyle. Use questions that have previously been prepared by your students. Ask your interviewee to address your students by name when possible. Later in class, show students the video of the interview and draw attention to any useful language that is used.

2 Do the same as above but make use of a video chat application (Skype, Facetime, etc.) to conduct the interview outside class time and use screencast software to record it for class.

Try this ☞ **Vocabulary interview**

Compile a list of vocabulary items (individual words, collocations, phrases, idioms, etc.) that you would like your students to revise. Set up a video camera on a subject – a British or American friend, for example – and go through the list, one item at a time. Ask your subject questions that will clarify, reinforce, or provide an alternative view on the use and semantics of the items in question (see Video 5.6 as an example). Good questions include:

● What would you call this? What would a British person/American call this?
● Do you use the idiom ...? Can you give an example of when or how you would use it?
● Which would you say is more common ...?
● How do you pronounce ...?

When you play the video in class, you may want to create a listening task for your students. However, this may not be necessary: as long as the audio is clear, learning benefits can be immediately obvious and students will often be motivated enough to listen.

↓ STAFFROOM VOX POPS

Vox pops (or *vox populi*) are sometimes referred to as 'man or woman on the street' interviews. They generally involve an interviewer roaming public spaces with a microphone and a camera operator, looking for willing subjects to answer questions about issues of the day.

Vox pop interviews are usually very short. During news broadcasts, they are often played in succession, with one interviewee's thoughts following another's.

The vox pop format is perfect for the language classroom. A simple question can be asked to a number of subjects. Often, answers will be diverse, but the language can be predictable and useful for the classroom.

Of course, it would be too time-consuming and impractical for any teacher to go onto the street and interrogate members of the public. However, the school staffroom can be a fantastic place for conducting quick interviews with colleagues just before going into class. Make sure that they aren't too busy or stressed before you bother them!

Creating your own content

Try this ☞ **Staffroom vox pops**

Choose a language point from your coursebook and consider a question that would lead to its production. Any of the following would work:

Question	Language point
What are you doing at the weekend?	Present continuous to talk about future plans (could also include *have to, probably will*, etc.)
What did you do at the weekend?	Past simple
What would you do if you won the lottery?	Second conditional
How are you?	Responses to a common question: (*I'm fine, great, not bad, I've been better, I can't complain*, etc.)
How many different countries have you visited?	Present perfect
What do you want for Christmas?	Would like

TABLE 5.1   *Examples of questions eliciting language points*

Watch Video 5.7 as an example. In class the video would be a perfect way to introduce the language point in question.

Part 3   Using video in the classroom

6   Basics

There are six main reasons for using online video in the language classroom:

1 Motivation

Video can be a particularly engaging medium for everyone in the classroom – teachers and students alike. A well-chosen video will lend itself to activities that maintain student curiosity and interest. And the more interesting the material, the more memorable the language learned in conjunction with it.

2 Language input

Learners need samples of language to study, process, adopt, and acquire. Video is an excellent resource for monologues and dialogues which, in turn, offer a rich source of grammar, lexis, and discourse, especially for spoken English. Chapter 8 is dedicated to spoken texts that are associated with online video.

3 Language output

Using video can provide a stimulus for language production tasks. As well as speaking and writing activities, we will also see a number of ways in which video can be used to elicit grammar and vocabulary from students.

4 Skills

Perhaps the most obvious skill that can be developed through video is listening. The internet is a repository of diverse English dialects and accents – both native and non-native. Through video, students can be trained to familiarize themselves with the sounds of English that they are most likely to meet and work with. However, there are other skills associated with video such as reading, critical thinking, and visual literacy.

5 Content

Online videos can be funny, entertaining, informative, or educational, and cater to virtually all interests. They can also be an invaluable resource for those of us who are required to teach other subjects through English (maths, psychology, media, art, geography, etc.). There is virtually no topic that is beyond the reach of online video.

6 Models

Finally, you might decide to make use of a short video to provide students with a model for their own work. For example, if you want students to create a video for homework in which they demonstrate how to make their favourite sandwich, you could show them an example from YouTube – there are many to choose from! As well as providing students with model language, the video can also serve to demonstrate technicalities associated with the filming and editing.

Working with video in the classroom means designing tasks which maximize student interaction with it. Here are five principles which aim for that:

1 Don't turn the classroom into a cinema

Avoid prolonged video viewing time in class. Students can do this at home. In addition, once students lose track, you lose their attention. Work with short videos. The shorter the video, the greater the challenge for us, the teachers, to consider ways of involving students with it.

2 Deconstruct the video

In Chapter 7, we will look at video deconstruction activities and techniques – silent viewing or audio only activities, for example. These involve isolating individual components of the video and presenting them to students before asking questions or setting tasks which require them to think about the bigger picture.

3 Don't be a slave to the spoken text

The majority of online videos were never created for language learning or teaching. As a result, spoken texts in video can be difficult for learners to understand. Individuals in the video may speak too fast or too quietly. Lexical choices can be obscure and low frequency. Grammar can be messy and non-standard. There can also be cultural references which add to the problem. In Chapter 8, we will look at ways to deal with these problems.

4 See beyond the spoken words

A video may provide us with language in the form of spoken words in the audio track, and these are the most obvious ones for language teachers to exploit. But video is much more versatile that that. Don't overuse video for listening activities. In Chapter 9, we will look at activities and techniques with a special focus on visual narratives.

Basics

5 Combine with other materials

Any online video may find itself at the heart of a network of other materials which are associated with it, either directly or indirectly (blog posts, websites, other videos, etc.). If we can identify these additional materials, we increase our possibilities for the classroom.

↓ TEXTS FROM VIDEO

Explicit and implicit texts

The next three chapters deal largely with texts (either written or spoken) that are associated with video. Texts can come directly from the video itself or from our students in response to it.

It can be useful to divide video texts into two categories: explicit and implicit.

Video text	Source	Examples
Explicit	Directly from the video: these are usually spoken texts from the audio, but also include subtitles and other onscreen texts.	monologues dialogues conversations presentations interviews narrations poems explanations titles and subtitles
Implicit	From the teacher or students in response to the video.	descriptions of people and things in the video descriptions of the narrative (i.e. what happens) descriptions of processes descriptions of what can be heard questions predictions analyses criticism

TABLE 6.1   *Examples of explicit and implicit video texts*

Explicit texts

The video gives us explicit texts directly. Most notably, these are the spoken texts that we hear – monologues, dialogues, and song lyrics, for example. But we also have to include onscreen texts such as subtitles. If the text can be transcribed directly from the video, then it is an explicit text.

Explicit texts can provide students with material for listening and reading as well as language for input and study.

Implicit texts

Implicit texts come from our own heads in response to the video. Whereas explicit texts are provided directly by the audio or screen, implicit texts come from the students or teacher.

When created by the teacher or materials writer, implicit texts can provide language input for students.

7 Deconstructing video

Two standard techniques

Consider either of the following classroom techniques:

Silent viewing: the teacher plays a video without sound and asks students to speculate about what the characters in the video are saying.

Audio only: the teacher lets students hear an audio track from a video but doesn't let them see the screen. Students have to guess what is happening in the video.

Both of these techniques involve deconstructing video and presenting students with isolated components of the medium. In each case, students interact with the isolated component, and use their imaginations, or understanding of the world, to create their own meaning.

A multimodal medium

Video is a multimodal medium – a dynamic interplay of moving images, editing techniques, graphics, music, sound effects, spoken words, onscreen text, and more. Different components of video work together and complement each other to co-construct meaning.

The following table shows the individual components that you can isolate for deconstruction activities and techniques.

	Video component
Audio (what we hear)	spoken words
	non-verbal
Visual (what we see)	moving images
	stills
Texts (what we read)	transcribed spoken words
	transcribed onscreen texts
	titles

TABLE 7.1 *Individual components for deconstruction activities*

Let's examine these individual components one at a time.

Deconstructing video

On page 19 we looked at ways of temporarily disabling the display of a classroom projector. By doing this, it is possible to isolate the audio track and create activities in which students can hear people speaking without seeing them.

When students hear the audio only, they are denied a vital part of the meaning of the video. For example, listen to Video 7.1 without looking at your screen. Consider what questions come to mind as you do so.

The obvious question would probably be: Why are people laughing? What is it that they can see that I can't? Even if you were able to hear every word clearly, there is no way that you can be sure what is amusing about the video. You will have had to make use of your imagination to speculate. By withholding the visual component in this way, you can engage students with the video.

Try this ☞ **What's going on?**

Play a video so that your students can hear it but can't see it. Allow them to write down any words or phrases that they hear. Put students into groups to share and compare what they heard and understood. Ask them to hypothesize about what is going on before showing them the video.

Try this ☞ **Adjectives of emotion**

Dictate a list of adjectives to your learners such as bored, angry, annoyed, relaxed, nervous, surprised, tired, excited, upset, confused, etc. Play a video in which people are speaking but don't let your students see the visual. Ask students to circle the adjectives which they think best describe the people's emotions (they can add their own if they like). Later, play the video – perhaps students' ideas will change when they see it.

Try this ☞ **Dialogues and conversations**

Choose a video in which more than one person is speaking. Play the video so that your students can hear it but can't see it. Ask questions such as:

- How many people can you hear?
- Who do you think they are?
- Where do you think they are?
- How old do you think they are?
- What are they talking about?
- What do you think their relationship is?

Show the video to your students and let them check their answers.

Try this ☞ **A celebrity speaks English**

Choose a video in which a celebrity speaks English. This could be a native or a non-native speaker of English. Play the video so that students hear the audio only. Ask them if they can guess who the celebrity is and what is going on. An example would be Video 7.2, in which the Prince of Wales (Prince Charles – Queen Elizabeth II's son) reads the weather forecast.

Deconstructing video

A note about listening skills

An isolated audio track can be great for creating student curiosity. It can be used to engage students with the spoken words in the video. It can also be used to get students speaking, as they speculate about the bigger picture.

However, isolated audio tracks are not always ideal for developing listening skills or for testing listening comprehension. Whole-video viewing may work better for those purposes.

As mentioned above, when you deny students the visual component of the video, you deny them a vital part of its meaning. Video is a multimodal medium, designed to be simultaneously seen and heard. The visual component is often essential for comprehension.

There are additional problems: audio quality can be bad, or background noise can interfere. There are also the problems associated with authentic language that were mentioned briefly above. These will be discussed in more detail in Chapter 8.

↓ THE AUDIO: NON-VERBAL

Audio tracks are often rich in non-verbal sounds which can be exploited in the classroom. These include background and ambient sounds, sound effects, laughter, applause, and music. All of these contribute to the meaning of the video.

The non-verbal background sounds are essential to the construction of the narrative. To appreciate this, play Video 7.3 with your eyes closed and listen to what you hear. As you do so, try to visualize the narrative and consider what is happening.

Try this ☞ **Collaborative storybuilding**

Choose a short video in which the non-verbal sounds contribute to the narrative or the story. Play the video so that your students can hear it but can't see it. Put students into pairs or small groups and ask them to make notes of all the things that they heard (or think they heard). Ask them to speculate about what is going on in the video before working together to visualize and construct a narrative by speaking or writing. You may want to offer a suggestion for how students begin (e.g. *A man walks into a shop* ...).

Try this ☞ **Modality**

Listen to a video without watching the screen and speculate about it. Create a list of sentences to express possibility, probability, and deduction, such as:

- David and Matthew are definitely not in the street.
- They're almost certainly in a shop.
- It might/could be a stationery shop.
- It can't be a supermarket because it's too quiet.
- Maybe David is the shopkeeper and Matthew is the customer.
- David is probably older than Matthew.
- They must know each other because they refer to each other by first names.

Play the video so that your students can hear it but can't see it. Write the sentences on the board and ask students to copy them into their books and decide whether or not they agree with them. If students don't agree with a sentence, they should amend it accordingly. Later, you could play a different video (Video 7.1 for example, again, audio only) and ask students to write similar sentences of their own.

Try this  **What do you hear?**

Choose a clip which contains a number of non-verbal sounds. Write down as many things that you can identify and then add some ideas of your own to the list. It might look like this:

- someone playing the drums
- someone eating spaghetti
- someone sneezing
- a dog barking
- someone playing table tennis
- a squeaky toy
- someone brushing their teeth
- a cat meowing
- someone speaking on the telephone
- someone chopping onions.

Give the list to your students and play the video so that they can hear it but can't see it. Ask students to choose the sounds from the list that they hear. Ask them to compare answers and then watch the video. A good video to use for this would be Video 7.4 – an advertisement that was created for an Italian sound production company. Note the grammar point which lends itself very well to this type of activity (noun + -ing).

Try this  **Why are they laughing?**

Choose a video which features audience laughter – a comedy sketch, for example. Let students hear the video without seeing it. Ask them to guess or hypothesize about the funny thing that is happening. This could be turned into a game of Twenty Questions (students have to work out the answer by asking you questions to which you can only answer *yes* or *no*.)

✓ **Getting it right**

QR codes and mobile devices

When using deconstruction activities, you can often avoid the need for a projector if students have access to mobile devices and wireless internet in class. For example, after playing an isolated audio track on the classroom computer, give out QR codes (see page 40) and ask students to access the video on their own devices.

↓ THE VISUAL: MOVING IMAGES

By turning the sound down, or by pressing the mute button on the computer keyboard, you can isolate the visual track and create activities for silent viewing.

One advantage of silent viewing is that you can design tasks in which the teacher or students speak while the video is playing.

Deconstructing video

Try this 👉 **Communal viewing**

Play a video with the sound down and make intermittent use of the pause button while asking questions about the visual content. Questions can be used to prepare students for listening. They can be used to elicit or introduce key language and ideas which they will later hear in the audio track. Alternatively, they can be used to encourage students to share their own knowledge about things that they see. This technique requires careful planning. For example, if you wanted to use Video 7.5, a nature documentary clip, you could use the plan shown below.

Pause moment	Question	Possible answer(s)
0:05	Do you know who this man is?	David Attenborough (the face and voice of British natural history programmes)
0:08	Do you know what animal this is?	A sloth
0:16	Why doesn't the sloth run away from David?	They are incredibly slow. They are also half-deaf and half-blind.
0:16	Where do you think this was shot?	The Costa Rican jungle
0:25	What do you know about sloths? What do they eat?	They eat leaves.
0:30	Why do you think sloths are so slow?	Because leaves are not very nutritious and the sloth compensates for that not by eating more but by doing less.
0:45	What's it doing?	Hanging around
1:05	It's going somewhere. Where do you think it's going and what do you think it's going to do?	It's going to defecate.
1:20	Why do you think it goes to the ground to defecate?	Students will find out when they hear the narration.
1:33	Can you think of any reasons why it is a bad idea to defecate on the ground?	The sloth is helpless on the ground. Any predator could attack it and it doesn't have the speed to escape.

TABLE 7.2   *A communal viewing plan*

Photocopiable © Oxford University Press

Try this 👉 **Providing narration**

Show students a natural history clip with the sound down. Ask them to write a narration to go over the top of it.

Try this 👉 **Dubbing a video**

Choose a video in which people are speaking. Film scenes where people use functional or predictable language work well for this (ordering in a restaurant, making telephone calls, meeting old friends in the street by chance, etc.). Play the video with the sound down and ask students to guess what the people are saying. You could ask them to attempt to lip-read if possible. Put students into pairs or groups and ask them to write a dialogue. Once you have offered corrections and language help, ask volunteers to act out their dialogues while the video plays with muted sound. In this way, they provide the protagonists with a voice. Do not ask students to synchronize their mouth movements with those of the people in the video – this is notoriously difficult. Later, students can listen to the audio and compare their ideas with what they actually hear.

Try this ☞ **The week's news**

Choose a current video news report, play it in class with the sound down and ask students to compare everything they know about the story before watching it with the sound up.

↓ THE VISUAL: STILLS

There are no moving images without non-moving images. Motion pictures consist of a series of individual frames. Any of these individual frames or **stills** can be exploited in the classroom.

You can do a lot with video stills. Tasks and activities will depend on the video that you select and the moment at which you obtain the still(s).

✓ *Getting it right*

Creating stills

There are two ways to obtain a still from a video. The first is quite simply to make use of the pause button to freeze the frame. The second is to pause the video at the frame you want and create an image file using screenshot software (see page 38).

Try this ☞ **Predictions and explanations**

Use stills as a way to engage students with a video by asking any of these questions:

- What happens next?
- What happened before?
- How did this situation come about?

Try this ☞ **Linking two stills**

Use screen capture software to isolate two images from the same video clip. Make prints of them, show them to your students and explain that they are individual frames from the same video. Ask students to guess or predict what happens in the video to connect the two images.

↓ TEXTS: TRANSCRIBED SPOKEN WORDS

Video is usually associated with activities that involve watching or listening. However, when you isolate spoken language from the audio and present it as text on paper, you can see that video lends itself particularly well to activities that involve reading. The following piece of narration has been transcribed from a video. As you read it, consider the questions that form in your mind:

If you've learned a lot about leadership and making a movement, then let's watch a movement happen, start to finish, in under three minutes, and dissect some lessons:

First, of course, a leader needs the guts to stand alone and look ridiculous. But what he's doing is so simple, it's almost instructional. This is key. You must be easy to follow.

Now here comes the first follower with the crucial role: he publicly shows everyone else how to follow. Notice how the leader embraces him as an equal, so it's not about the leader any more – it's about them, plural. Notice how he's calling to his friends to join in. It takes guts to be a first follower. You stand out and brave ridicule, yourself. Being a first follower is an under-appreciated form of leadership. The first follower transforms a lone nut into a leader. If the leader is the flint, the first follower is the spark that really makes the fire.

Now here's the second follower. This is a turning point: it's proof that the first has done well. Now it's not a lone nut, and it's not two nuts. Three is a crowd and a crowd is news.

A movement must be public. Make sure outsiders see more than just the leader. Everyone needs to see the followers, because new followers emulate followers – not the leader.

Now here come two more people, then three more immediately. Now we've got momentum. This is the tipping point and now we have a movement. As more people jump in, it's no longer risky. If they were on the fence before, there's no reason not to join in now. They won't stand out. They won't be ridiculed. And they will be part of the in-crowd if they hurry. Over the next minute you'll see the rest who prefer to stay part of the crowd, because eventually they'd be ridiculed for not joining.

As you read these words, you will probably find yourself asking a number of questions which could include:

- What is going on here?
- What is the event/movement that is being narrated?
- Who is the leader and what is he doing?
- How does the first follower publicly show his support?
- Why would it be risky to join in?
- What is the genre of this video (a nature documentary, an advertisement, a presentation, etc.)?

Such questions seem to arise quite naturally. Perhaps in some cases, your imagination or your knowledge of the world was able to suggest answers. Or perhaps not! All should become clear when you watch Video 7.6, a well-known viral video to which entrepreneur Derek Sivers added his own commentary.

Try this ☞ **Questions from the teacher**

Transcribe a text from a video and think of some questions that will encourage students to engage with it before watching. Note that it is often not possible to comprehend an isolated video text without seeing the video. If this is the case, the questions aren't really comprehension questions. They serve to get students speculating about the video, making predictions, and using their own world knowledge. They involve intensive reading and higher-order thinking skills.

Try this ☞ **Questions from the students**

Give your students a short text and tell them that it is a transcript from a video. Instead of presenting them with questions that you have prepared, ask them to construct their own, which they can then ask you in an attempt to work out what is happening in the video.

Try this 👉 **Missing word**

In some cases, a transcribed spoken text can be turned into a puzzle if you omit a single word from it. For example, in the following text, the same word has been removed twice. The students' task is to guess what the mystery creature is.

> **Mystery creature**
> This recently-discovered colony of _____ (plural noun) is unlike any other. They don't need to huddle together every winter for protection against the bitter cold because these little fellows can do something that no other _____ (singular noun) can. Isn't that amazing? And how do they use this incredible ability? Well, they fly thousands of miles to the rain forests of South America where they spend the winter basking in the tropical sun.

The video text is taken from Video 7.7, which was released by the BBC on April 1st 2008 (April Fools' Day).

Try this 👉 **A single line**

Instead of giving students an entire transcript, give them just a very small excerpt from it. This could be a single statement, exclamation, utterance, or an exchange between two people. For example:

> We're going to open the door right now. It's a little bit like opening up the door to another world.

Ask students questions which require them to think about the bigger picture and construct a narrative. In this case, you could ask:

- Whose words are these?
- Where is the door?
- Is the door real or is it metaphorical?
- What is behind it?

After eliciting as many examples as possible, show students Video 7.8, which was filmed inside the McMurdo Station, a research centre located in the Antarctic. The door in question is opened to give the viewer a glimpse of a particularly ferocious storm outside.

Note that this technique can be effective for introducing a language point that is contained within the chosen excerpt. For example, in the case above you could choose *going to* for a planned imminent action, or the common spoken chunk *a (little) bit like* which means *similar to*.

↓ TEXTS: TRANSCRIBED ONSCREEN TEXTS

Subtitles

Subtitles are perhaps the most obvious type of onscreen text associated with video. These are often used to duplicate or translate spoken words for the purpose of comprehension. However, subtitles can also be used as an integral part of the meaning of the video.

Deconstructing video

For example, in a video entitled *The Rings of the Earth* (Video 7.9), animator Roy Prol uses short subtitle-like texts to complement his moving images of our planet and describe what it would look like if it had a ring system like Saturn's.

On page 52, we looked at kinetic typography, a technique which has given onscreen life to countless speeches, radio broadcasts, song lyrics, film dialogues, and other texts. Another popular kinetic typography video is *29 Ways to Stay Creative*, by Japanese motion graphic design studio TO-FU (Video 7.10).

IMAGE 7.1   *Still from 29 Ways to Stay Creative*

Isolating an onscreen text

Isolating an onscreen text is simple. Simply copy it and give it to students in non-video format (on paper, on the blackboard, etc.). You then have a number of options.

Try this ☞   **Word choice activity**

Isolate an onscreen text and use it for the basis of a word choice activity (see example below). After completing the activity, let students correct their own work by showing them the video.

If our planet had a ring system like Saturn's: The rings would be aligned with the Earth's **equator/poles** *(1), and they would appear across the sky from* **east to west/ north to south** *(2).*

Near the equator, the rings would appear **thick/thin** *(3) and* **perpendicular/ parallel** *(4) to the poles. But far from the equator, the rings would appear much* **thinner/thicker** *(5) and close to the horizon.*

The rings would appear **bright/dull** *(6) in the night sky, because they would* **reflect/absorb** *(7) the Sun's light, exactly as the moon does.*

Try this ☞   **Dictation**

Dictate a short onscreen text to your students before playing the video. When they watch the video, the text will come to life and students will be able to check what they have written.

Try this ☞ **Gap fill**

Isolate an onscreen text and use it for the basis of a gap-fill activity. After completing the activity, let students correct their own work by showing them the video. The example below makes use of a selection of suggestions from *29 Ways to Stay Creative* (Video 7.10). Students' task is to consider possible verbs that could go in the gaps (a single word per gap).

_____ lists

_____ a notebook everywhere

_____ away from the computer

_____ breaks

_____ in the shower

_____ to new music

_____ yourself with creative people

Don't _____ up

Allow yourself to _____ mistakes

_____ somewhere new

_____ lots of rest

_____ risks

_____ the rules

_____ your workspace

_____ fun

_____ something

↓ TITLES

Sometimes the title of a video will explicitly tell us what we are going to see (e.g. *Baby elephant sneezes and scares himself*). Usually, however, titles are more subtle than that. They can imply what the video is about, and make us curious to click on the link (e.g. *The most useless machine ever*). There are a number of ways in which you can exploit ambiguous titles.

Try this ☞ **What are you going to see?**

Choose an intriguing video title and write it on the board. Any of the following examples would work:

- *The most useless machine ever*
- *Clumsy best man ruins our wedding*
- *The train that never stops at a station*
- *29 ways to stay creative*
- *Human skateboard.*

Ask students to speculate on what they are going to see before showing them the video. For example, what is the nature of the useless machine? How does the clumsy best man ruin the wedding? How could a passenger train not have to stop at a station? How many ways of staying creative can you predict? What is a human skateboard and how does it work? This technique can be used to engage students with a video and/or get them talking.

Try this 👉 **Grammar Hangman**

Choose a video title which contains a grammar point that you would like to study. For example, if you wanted to teach reflexive pronouns, you could choose either of the following:

- *Girl takes picture of herself every day for three years*
- *Baby elephant sneezes and scares himself.*

Draw a numbered grid on the board that corresponds to the title. Each line should represent one word in the title.

Show students the video and tell them that the grid refers to its title. Ask them to suggest individual words – one at a time – that fit onto the grid (you may have to give them a word or two to get started). For each suggested word, students should also give you the numbered position onto which it should be placed. Write correct answers on the board. Each time a student gives an incorrect answer – either an incorrect word or an incorrect position – add an extra part to the Hangman diagram. Make a note of all incorrect guesses on the board so that students don't repeat them.

Students win if they successfully manage to identify the whole title before you draw the complete Hangman figure.

↓ A FORMULA

Many of the deconstruction activities and techniques that have been suggested in this chapter involve a basic three-step formula. This is:

1 Stimulus (possible language input)	Students are given an isolated video component. This involves one of the following: They read or listen to a text. They see images.
2 Exploration (possible language output)	Students consider questions or do tasks which require them to visualize, imagine, or hypothesize about the bigger picture.
3 Comparison (or resolution)	Students watch the video and compare their answers with what they see.

TABLE 7.3   *A basic three-step formula for deconstruction activities*

Why this works

Video is a complex medium. Different layers of the medium work together to co-construct meaning. When we take these layers apart and build them up gradually, meaning emerges. This slow release approach can be effective for the following reasons.

1 It keeps students curious.

2 It heightens the impact of the video and can be memorable.

3 It involves multiple meetings with a text. For example, you might give students a transcribed monologue, and then let them hear the audio. Finally they watch the whole video. With each meeting with the text,

students experience it with a new layer of meaning. Each of these steps requires intensive, holistic, in-depth processing of the language.

4   When we isolate a video component, questions which require students to think about the bigger picture often emerge quite naturally (e.g. *What are they talking about? What are they referring to?*, etc.)

5   The exploration step can involve lateral thinking, visualization, problem solving, and other higher-order thinking skills. Contrast this with the simple comprehension-style questions that so often accompany reading texts.

↓ MATERIALS COMBINATION

No complete video will ever offer the full picture. In order to appreciate the bigger story, we have to go beyond the video and find additional components – other materials that are directly or indirectly associated with it. By identifying and sourcing complementary materials, our options for the classroom increase.

Try this ☞ **Syllabus complementation**

For any video that you would like to use in class, consider how you can integrate it into your syllabus or coursebook. Consider language points that you need to cover. Can any of these be illustrated by the video that you want to work with? Alternatively, consider topics that you need to cover and consider how a video could be included. For example, the video in which Prince Charles reads the weather forecast (Video 7.2) could be used for any of the following:

● As a way of illustrating *will* for predictions
● To introduce or enhance topics such as Scotland, the weather, the BBC, or royalty.

Try this ☞ **Newspaper articles**

Videos regularly find themselves at the heart of news stories. For example, a controversial advertisement could make the headlines after receiving a particularly high number of viewer complaints. In such a situation, find the advertisement online, show it to students, and ask them to guess or identify the controversy and say why they think it is controversial. Then distribute a newspaper article that explains the controversy, before asking students to discuss the question.

Try this ☞ **Realia**

Look for ways of enhancing students' experience of a video by making use of objects which appear in them. For example, by introducing students to a toy penguin, you could elicit things that penguins can and cannot do, before showing them the BBC April Fool's Day video mentioned earlier (see Video 7.7).

Try this ☞ **Images**

Make use of photographs, illustrations, artwork, cartoons, maps, or other images that can be used in combination with a video. For example, show students a satellite image of Antarctica and ask them if they are familiar with it.

After establishing that it is Antarctica, ask students what they might see if they could suddenly open a door onto the icy continent. After eliciting ten things, show the Antarctica video mentioned above (Video 7.8). Note that you may accept penguins, but not polar bears, as an answer.

Try this ☞ **Wikipedia pages**

Wikipedia is a great source of texts which can be used in combination with video clips. For example, after using *The Rings of the Earth* (Video 7.9), students could be referred to Wikipedia to find six facts about Saturn's ring system.

Try this ☞ **Websites**

It is always worth looking for resources on websites that are associated with online videos. For example, the BBC Nature website is a great resource for wildlife news, facts, and photographs. It could be used to supplement an activity on the sloth, for example.

Try this ☞ **Investigate a CV**

Students of business English can be asked to explore the professional backgrounds of the people behind popular online video series. For this, they can make use of networking sites such as *LinkedIn* to build up a professional's profile.

Try this ☞ **Complementing videos**

For any video that you want to use, consider whether there are any others that could be used in combination. For example, there is another online video from the BBC, which shows how the flying penguins video was made (Video 7.11).

8　Using spoken texts

If speaking is the most important skill, then samples of spoken language are surely the most important source of language input. And as video grows as an everyday medium of communication, so do the number of spoken texts at our disposal.

A well-chosen video will provide students with language that they can adopt, acquire, and make their own. It can also be used to study features of spoken English and discourse.

In this chapter, we will focus on spoken texts which are associated with video. We will look at monologues and dialogues which are either scripted, semi-scripted, or unscripted.

↓ POTENTIAL PROBLEMS

Most online videos were not created for language learning and many may present students with comprehension problems. These include:

- cultural references
- slang
- low-frequency language items
- non-standard grammar
- dialects
- strong accents
- poor quality audio recording equipment
- distracting background noises
- speech that is too fast, too quiet, or unclear.

As teachers, we have to be aware of problems like these when selecting videos for the classroom and designing activities around them. When things go wrong, students can be quick to blame themselves. Rather than appreciating that a spoken text can be inherently difficult to understand, they may doubt their own comprehension abilities. The unintended result can be demotivated students.

Of course, comprehension problems can also affect us, the teachers. During the lesson planning stage, we may want to transcribe a spoken text for our students. If a part of it is unintelligible, we have to decide how to deal with it. One option is mentioned later in this chapter (see page 95).

1 Whole video viewing

Meaningful video comprehension involves simultaneous processing of the audio and the visual. For teachers who are intent on developing or testing students' comprehension skills, whole video viewing is the most natural approach. Student comprehension can also be enhanced through the use of subtitles.

In some cases, though, visuals can actually distract from the spoken words. This could be the case for a fast-moving movie trailer, for example.

2 Audio only

This approach was mentioned in Chapter 7. By presenting students with the audio only, we can maintain curiosity and ask questions which require them to engage with the spoken text and consider the bigger picture (who is speaking, where they are, etc.). Students can also hear verbal punctuation, such as pauses, phrasing, and intonation.

Remember, however, that by denying students the visual component, we deny them an essential part of the meaning of the video. For this reason, we should be wary about using isolated audio tracks to test students' listening skills.

3 Transcripts

This approach was also mentioned in Chapter 7. By transcribing a spoken text, you can create activities that involve intensive reading and encourage students to speculate about missing information – information that would be provided by the audio or visual component.

Reading is generally easier than listening. Students have control: they can see every word on the paper. They can reread parts of the text as and when they want to. They can take their time to process the language. In addition, when words are transcribed, students are no longer at the mercy of poor quality audio and distracting background noises.

On the other hand, when using isolated transcripts, students are denied the audio as well as the visual component. Words on paper can be flat, black and white, and lifeless. They lack the layer of meaning that the audio offers.

But, as we will see, one of the great advantages of using transcripts of spoken texts is that the language can be adapted. In other words, what we hear in the video does not have to be the same as what we read on paper.

Note that there are a number of video sites that offer spoken text transcripts (see Appendix 1).

↓ MEANING EMERGENCE

When designing video activities that involve spoken texts, you can stage the lesson so that meaning emerges gradually while student curiosity is maintained. Here are three example approaches:

- Students listen to an isolated audio track, then read the transcript, and later watch the whole video.
- Students read a transcript, then listen to the isolated audio track, and later watch the whole video.
- Students simultaneously read a transcript and listen to the isolated audio track, and later watch the whole video.

Let's look at three examples of spoken texts from video. In each case, we will consider possible uses for them, as well as potential problems and suggested solutions.

↓ EXAMPLE ONE: A NON-SCRIPTED MONOLOGUE

IMAGE 8.1   *Still from Baby Armadillo*

In <u>Video 8.1</u>, we are introduced to a nine-banded armadillo by Texan blogger, David Werst. A transcript of the video is included below. As you watch the video and then read the transcript, consider whether or not you would use it in your classroom. If so, what would you do with it?

OK, for those of you who've never seen an armadillo up close, this is, uh, a baby Texas, uh, nine-banded armadillo and you can count the bands – one – two – three – four – five – six – seven – eight – nine – and, uh, he's not as colorful as some. But you might notice his feet – these feet are made for digging. If you'll watch these feet, uh, he can, uh … they're just like little shovels. They can dig in and out of anything like that. Uh, even though they do have big ears, uh, they can't hear very good. I actually snuck up on this one and, uh, grabbed him and I've grabbed big adults like that too. Uh, but, uh, whenever you put them down – I mean – they're, they can dig and take off. They get a lot of traction with these, with these toes. Uh, but they, uh – and they're pretty quick. They can also jump right straight up. And I've got a dog coming over here so I'm going to have to lift him up. [laughs] Uh, but uh, they are cute little rascals but they can do a lot of damage, uh, to the yard. They eat grubs and worms and all kinds of things. But, uh, this is, uh, this is what they look like. Hi y'all. How are you? Welcome to Texas. OK – we're going to go release this one somewhere other than our yard. Uh, we have a lot of armadillos here but I don't like them in the yard all that much.

Potential problems

First of all, let's consider some potential problems with the spoken text.

1 Students may find it difficult to understand David's West Texan accent.

2 David uses some natural features of the Texan dialect which could be considered non-standard (e.g. 'they can't hear very good' rather than 'very well' and 'hi y'all' rather than 'hi everyone'.) We probably wouldn't want students to acquire this language.

3 Transcribed spoken language can look very messy on paper. David's transcript illustrates some common features of spoken language such as fillers ('uh', 'I mean'), false starts ('they're, they can dig and take off') and repetition ('But, uh, this is, uh, this is what they look like.') Some teachers may feel that students should be protected from this sort of thing.

4 Even native speakers make mistakes! David should have referred to the animal as a 'Texan nine-banded armadillo' rather than a 'Texas nine-banded armadillo'.

5 Texts especially created for language learners often contain multiple illustrative examples of language points (multiple examples of present perfect structures, for example). A text like this does not, and we may be unsure of how to use it to teach language.

Advantages

On the other hand, David's spoken text has a lot to offer:

1 Many people would find armadillos interesting.

2 David communicates well. His text is well-structured and he speaks clear, West Texan English. Background sounds in the video do not really interfere with his words.

3 The text has approximately 250 words. That's a convenient length for teaching.

4 David's text contains some useful language that we might want students to acquire.

5   Although it might be difficult for students to understand David's West Texan accent, we could use the video to draw attention to features of it, and broaden students' appreciation of the variety of sounds that exist in English.

6   Similarly, although we probably wouldn't want students to adopt features of David's Texan dialect, a text like this can be valuable for demonstrating the fact that English exists in many varieties.

7   On page 141, we will see an activity in which students capture their own spoken texts on video, and then transcribe their own words. In such situations, it is important that students do not judge their communicative abilities solely by the way that their words look on paper. David's armadillo text would reassure students that on paper, unscripted speech naturally looks untidy compared with the written texts that we are used to. It could also be reassuring for them to know that even native speakers make mistakes!

Adapting spoken texts

Transcribed video texts can be altered or adapted. With our students in mind, there are many reasons why we might decide to make changes and there are many types of changes that we can make. For example, you could decide to:

- simplify parts of the transcript
- tidy up parts of the transcript
- shorten parts of the transcript
- omit parts of the transcript
- remove cultural references that students are unfamiliar with
- choose not to include parts which are unintelligible
- change non-standard language to standard language
- change low-frequency words or phrases to higher-frequency choices
- swap words, phrases, or grammar choices for others that your students have recently met and give them a chance to revise them
- swap words, phrases, or grammar choices for others that you need to teach.

An adapted transcript

Below is an example adapted transcript. The specific changes made will almost certainly be different to the ones that you would choose. They reflect a particular approach, teaching aim, and specific students.

Note that the key word has been omitted three times. This allows students to read the text and guess what the mystery animal is (after clarifying a number of language items such as *shovels*, *to creep up on*, *traction*, *grubs*, etc.).

OK, for those of you who've never seen an _____ , this is a baby nine-banded _____ and you can count the bands: one – two – three – four – five – six – seven – eight – nine. He's not as colourful as some. But you might notice his feet – these feet are made for digging. They're just like little shovels.

Even though they do have big ears, they can't hear very well. I actually sneaked up on this one and grabbed him and I've grabbed big adults like that too. But if I put him down, he'll escape. They get a lot of traction with those toes. And they're pretty quick. They can also jump quite high. And I've got a dog coming over here so I'm going to have to lift him up. They are cute little things but they can do a lot of damage to the yard. They eat grubs and worms and things like that. But this is what they look like. 'Hello. How are you? Welcome to Texas.' OK – we're going to go and release this one somewhere outside our yard. We have a lot of _____ here but I don't like them in the yard all that much.

Photocopiable © Oxford University Press

Why this works

As long as you maintain the essential meaning of the video, students will rarely notice that you have used an adapted transcript, especially if they aren't simultaneously reading and listening. If students do realize that the transcript has been adapted, this shouldn't present a problem. Just be honest and explain your reasons for making changes.

Try this ☞ **Dialects and features of spoken language**

Let students compare a tidy transcript such as the one above with the actual spoken words in the audio. Ask them to look for differences between the two texts. This can be a good way of drawing attention to non-standard structures, language choices, and slang. It can also draw attention to aspects of spoken language, such as fillers, false starts and inconsistencies (the fact that David refers to the armadillo as both 'him' and 'it'.)

Try this ☞ **Accents**

Choose a video in which a speaker has an interesting accent. Transcribe the words and give out copies of the transcript. Once students have familiarized themselves with the text, play the video and ask them to listen carefully to the sounds that they hear. Write the following questions on the board:

- Do you know what accent this is?
- Can you identify any notable sounds, features, or characteristics of it?
- Can you hear any sounds that you have never heard before in English?
- Can you hear any familiar sounds being used in unexpected places?
- Do you detect any notable or unusual use of intonation?

Play the video a number of times and encourage students to choose a phrase that they like and imitate it. For example, students might like to count to ten using a West Texan accent in the way that David does in his video.

Try this ☞ **Use excerpts**

Isolate a number of excerpts from a spoken text. Adapt these if necessary and dictate them to your learners. In the following example, students could guess what the mystery animal is, or draw a picture of how they imagine it to look before watching the video:

- They've got nine bands across their bodies.
- Their feet are made for digging.
- Even though they have big ears, they can't hear very well.
- They get a lot of traction with their toes.
- They're pretty quick.
- They can also jump quite high.
- They are cute little things but they can do a lot of damage.
- They eat grubs and worms and things like that.

IMAGE 8.2   *Drawings of the mystery animal by Robert, aged 34, and Ingrid, aged 32*

Try this 👉   **Pushing and pulling**

As mentioned above, authentic texts often lack multiple examples of language points for study. One way to get around that is to use the push and pull technique: start by selecting six language items from the text that you think will be most beneficial for your students. These can be words, phrases, collocations, idioms, or grammatical structures. Then do the following:

1   Push the language: Tell your students that you have chosen six pieces of language from the text that you think they should take home with them. Present the language items one at a time, and explain your reasons for choosing them (usefulness, revision, etc.).
2   Pulling the language: Ask students to do the same – they should read the text again and choose six language items of their own that they want to take home. The items that students choose should be different to the ones that you gave them. Finally, let students compare and share their choices and explain their reasons for making them.

↓ EXAMPLE TWO: A NON-SCRIPTED DIALOGUE

In Chapter 5, we saw a video in which Jess and James philosophize over a question that I put to them (Video 5.5).

Potential problems

1   As you would expect, the second conditional arises naturally out of the question that Jess and James are asked. However, it does so inconsistently. For example, when James justifies his answer at the start of the video, he refuses to speak with a hypothetical voice. He says:

Because, a month in prison … you have company for a start. It's only a month long and you get adequate care taken of you. A desert island … you're left alone. You don't have that.

On the other hand, texts which are written for language learners will tend to illustrate a target language point consistently.

2 When people engage in conversation, they may interrupt each other, speak simultaneously, or finish each other's sentences. All of this means that transcribed dialogues look even more messy than transcribed monologues.

Advantages

1 Students could compare an adapted transcript with the language in the video and become aware of the inconsistencies mentioned above.

2 The video is a good demonstration of how meaning is co-constructed between more than one person during conversation. Jess and James work together to arrive at a consensual answer to the question: they build upon each other's ideas; they support each other and offer encouragement; they request justification and elaboration when necessary; they question each other's answers and disagree indirectly.

3 The language that Jess and James use would serve as a model for a collaborative second conditional speaking activity.

4 The spoken text is short and complete. Jess and James speak clearly.

An adapted transcript

What follows is an adapted version of the spoken text. As before, you might decide to adapt it differently. I have made the following changes:

1 I have tidied up the text to make it easier to read.

2 In order to make things consistent, I have added the hypothetical *would* when it was missing before.

3 I have changed the adjective *grim* for the higher-frequency *depressing*.

4 I have changed the adjective *ripped* for the higher frequency *fit*. (I had never heard the word *ripped* in that context until my meeting with Jess and James. Apparently, if you are ripped, you have well-developed muscles!)

5 I have not included my initial question. This provides a simple reading task – students read the text and work out what question Jess and James were asked.

James: Oh, a month in prison, definitely.
Jess: Why?
James: Because, you would have company in prison for a start. It would only be a month long and you would get adequate care. On a desert island, you would be left alone.
Jess: But that would be fun.
James: Well, it would be fun if you had adequate resources.
Jess: If I had enough books, I would definitely choose a desert island.

James:	What about water and food?
Jess:	Well, yeah. I wouldn't be very good at that.
James:	Plus, you would have to think about suncream. And you would get books in prison.
Jess:	Then I'd sit in the shade. I don't know. Hmm …
James:	What would be the problem with prison for you?
Jess:	It would just be a bit depressing. Like, at least if you were on an island, it would be nice and scenic.
James:	Yeah. And you'd feel like a free person.
Jess:	It'd be like a holiday. But then you wouldn't see anyone for two years and you'd probably go crazy.
James:	Two years is quite a long time …
Jess:	Yeah
James:	Whereas one month is …
Jess:	Maybe I'd pick prison as well.
James:	Yeah
Jess:	You'd also get really fit because you'd probably …
James:	… you'd work out all the time.
Jess:	Yeah
James:	Yeah, that's true.
Jess:	Really fit and really intelligent.
James:	Yeah. Well, you would only have a month.
Jess:	And you could write your memoirs.
James:	You would only have a month, Jess.
Jess:	Oh yeah

Photocopiable © Oxford University Press

Try this ☞ **Rewrite a transcript**

Give students a short tidy transcript and ask them to rewrite it so that it resembles real spoken language. Then let them watch the video and compare their answers.

Try this ☞ **What was the question?**

Play an interview video, but start it just after a question is asked. If you wanted to use Jess and James's video, for example, you would have to play it from 0:07. Students' listening task is to work out what the question was. The question could then be used as the basis of a grammar Hangman activity (see page 88). Alternatively, for an activity that involves reading, use a transcript such as the one above (the initial question is missing).

Try this ☞ **Who said what?**

Isolate a number of excerpts from a dialogue and ask students to recall or predict who says what. Excerpts could be chosen to illustrate a language point – the second conditional, for example:

- If I had enough books, I would definitely choose a desert island.
- You would have to think about suncream.
- You wouldn't see anyone for two years and you'd probably go crazy.
- You'd get really fit because you'd probably work out all the time.

A good script read by good actors will generally be tidier than non-scripted language and simpler to use in the language classroom. However, we still might want to make changes to the transcript.

Video 8.2 is from a BBC comedy series called *Walk on the Wild Side*. It consists of sketches in which comedians give voices to animals in clips which are taken from nature documentaries. Watch the monkeys (00:44 to 01:25) and decide how you would make use of the spoken text to teach.

Potential problems

1 The monkey dentist makes reference to a town in central England called Dudley. Since the series was created for a British audience, we are expected to be aware of Dudley. However, most people who are not from the UK will probably not be, and that could distract from the meaning.

2 It contains some slang terms such as *a cheeky little taste* and *rank*. Language like this can be strongly associated with specific groups of native speakers and would sound particularly strange coming from most learners of English.

3 It contains two examples of ellipsis in which unstressed words in question forms are not pronounced. If learners were to produce language like this in an exam situation, they would almost certainly lose marks.

   • Going anywhere nice on holiday? (Rather than: Are you going anywhere nice on holiday?)
   • You got kids? (Rather than: Have you got kids?)

Advantages

1 Most people find the clip quite funny.

2 The text is short and the language is clear.

3 It contains some useful language that you may want your students to acquire.

4 As before, we might want to point out features of spoken language in order to build on students' linguistic awareness.

5 With a few changes to the transcript, the text will lend itself to a number of language learning activities.

An adapted transcript

In the transcript below, I have made the following changes:

1 I have chosen to use only part of the text.

2 I have removed the reference to Dudley.

3   I have given the questions their full forms.

4   I have swapped the low-frequency structure *You could do with a filling* for the higher-frequency *You need a filling*.

5   I have swapped the dentist's question 'Is it mainly bananas you eat?' to 'Do you eat a lot of bananas?'

6   For consistency, I have phrased the dentist's requests in the same way in each case ('Please don't try to talk when my hands are in your mouth.').

Note that the spoken text lends itself to a natural task. Students could either listen to the audio or read the transcript and speculate on the following:

- Where are A and B?
- Who are they?
- What is going on here?

> **A:** If you'd just like to open wide, sir …
> **B:** OK.
> **A:** Are you going anywhere nice on your holidays?
> **B:** [Tries to talk but can't.]
> **A:** No, please don't try to talk when my hands are in your mouth, sir. Uh, my wife and I are thinking of going abroad this year – the UK. She's got family in the zoo over there. Have you got kids?
> **B:** [Tries to talk but can't.]
> **A:** Please don't try to talk when my hands are in your mouth, sir. You need a filling here at the back. Do you eat a lot of bananas?
> **B:** [Tries to talk but can't.]
> **A:** I won't ask you again, sir. Please don't try to talk when my hands are in your mouth.

Try this 👉 **Text memory game**

Give out copies of a short transcribed video text and tell students that you are going to play a memory game. Give them one minute to look at the text and pay attention to as many aspects of the language as possible. When time is up, ask students to hide their texts. Then ask questions which should require them to recall or reconstruct language within it. If you were using the monkey dentist text, for example, you could ask any of the following:

- The dentist asks the patient three questions. Can you remember what they are?
- The dentist uses the present continuous to talk about a future plan. Can you remember what he says?
- The dentist becomes impatient with the patient. Each time this happens, he says the same thing: 'Please don't …' (can you complete the request?)
- The dentist says that the patient needs something. What is the thing and where is it needed?

Try this ☞ **Acting out a script**

Give out copies of a short script. Put students into pairs or groups and tell them that they are actors. Give them some time to prepare for a performance (five minutes, for example). Then invite pairs of students to perform their interpretations of the script in front of the class. Finally show the video and let students compare their performances with those of the actors.

Try this ☞ **A single good example**

As has already been mentioned, texts that are not designed for language learning tend not to contain multiple examples of language for study. One way to exploit such texts is to look for a single good example to illustrate a language point. For example, the monkey dentist script contains a great case of the present continuous to talk about future plans. You could use this to introduce the language point before moving on to an activity in your coursebook. You could even use a meme generator to create an image for your classroom wall to keep the language in students' minds (see Appendix 7).

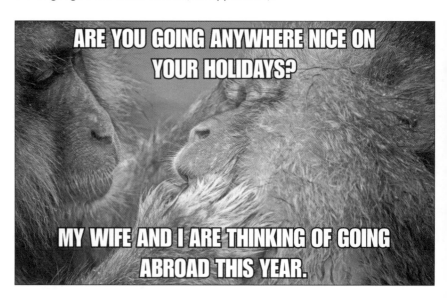

IMAGE 8.3 *A meme-generated video still*

9   Using video narratives

A video can tell a story without words. For example <u>Video 9.1</u> is an advertisement in which the moving pictures do most of the talking.

IMAGE 9.1   *Still from Home Sweet Home (CZAR.BE)*

One way to exploit a video like this is to first consider the implicit language that is associated with it. At the simplest level, this could be a list of the things that we see. For example: *a picnic table   a road   trees   a forest a meadow   grass   a horse   a river   a valley   rain   a lorry a lorry driver   a cup of tea   an envelope   a post box   a house*

Implicit texts and language can come either from the students or from the teacher.

Try this ☞   **What did you see?**

Ask students to write down as many things as they can while watching a video. Elicit their ideas and write the best ones on the board. This can be good for working with nouns and noun phrases, singular and plural forms, and articles (especially *a*, *an*, and the zero article).

Using video narratives

↓ DESCRIBING ACTIONS AND MOVEMENT

Videos or film clips which portray journeys, routines, chases, or action sequences can be useful for teaching language to describe actions and movement. In order to do this, we have to prepare a series of sentences which puts the visual narrative into words. If we were using the *Home Sweet Home* advertisement, for example, we could write the following:

1 He wakes up on a picnic table and realizes that he has been left behind.

2 He walks through a forest and almost slips while going down a steep slope.

3 He walks through a meadow and gets a fright when he sees a horse.

4 While he is running away from the horse, he trips over a stone.

5 He thinks about crossing a river.

6 He gets caught in the rain.

7 He hitches a ride with a friendly lorry driver.

8 They drive through a tunnel.

9 They stop at a diner.

10 He sees a photograph of the lorry driver's family and starts to feel homesick.

11 The lorry driver sends him home.

12 When he gets home, he goes to bed.

Note that it is very natural to describe video narratives using present tense structures.

Try this ☞ **Jumbled sentences**

Create a worksheet of jumbled sentences which relate to the things that happen in a video (*Home Sweet Home*, for example). Ask students to cut up the texts and put them into chronological order after watching the video.

- He sees a photograph of the lorry driver's family and starts to feel homesick.
- They drive through a tunnel.
- He walks through a forest and almost slips while going down a steep slope.
- He hitches a ride with a friendly lorry driver.
- When he gets home, he goes to bed.
- He walks through a meadow and gets a fright when he sees a horse.
- The lorry driver sends him home.
- While he is running away from the horse, he trips over a stone.
- He thinks about crossing a river.
- He gets caught in the rain.
- They stop at a diner.
- He wakes up on a picnic table and realizes that he has been left behind.

Photocopiable © Oxford University Press

Try this ☞ **Memory test**

After working with a step-by-step narrative text (see previous Try this idea), ask students to recall – from memory – everything that happened in the video. In doing so, they should convert present tense structures to past tense structures. For example:

1   He woke up on a picnic table.
2   He walked through a forest and almost slipped while going down a steep slope.
3   He walked through a meadow and got a fright when he saw a horse.
4   While he was running away from the horse, he tripped over a stone.

Note that we should be open to the idea that students may find alternative ways of expressing the things that happen in the video.

Try this 👉 **Screenshots**

Use screenshots (see below) from a video that your students have seen to introduce any of the following structures:

- Present perfect + *just*: *He has just woken up.*
- About to do something: *He is about to trip over a stone.*
- Present continuous: *He is thinking about crossing the river.*
- Going to do something: *They are going to stop at a diner.*

Once students are familiar with the images and the language that they are expected to produce in response to them, you could play a game. For example, put students into groups, show images, elicit language, and award points for correct answers.

a   b

c   d

IMAGE 9.2   *Fours stills from Home Sweet Home*

Try this 👉 **Observation test**

Tell students that you are going to test their power of observation. Play a video (in this case *Home Sweet Home*) and ask them to pay close attention to what they see. After viewing, dictate a number of sentences that relate to it – some true and some false (see examples below). If students think that a sentence is true, they should write it as they hear it. If they think that a sentence is false, they should correct it accordingly.

1 He wakes up on the ground.
2 He walks through a forest and almost slips while walking down a steep slope.
3 He walks past a shopping centre.
4 He walks through a meadow and gets a fright when he sees a cow.
5 He tries to make friends with the animal.
6 While he is running, he trips over a stick.
7 He gets caught in the rain.
8 He hitches a ride with a friendly lorry driver.
9 They drive across a bridge.
10 When he gets home, he brushes his teeth.

↓ PROCESSES

Videos which demonstrate step-by-step processes lend themselves very well to activities for the language classroom. Examples include the following:

- cookery videos
- how-it-works videos
- how-it-is-made videos
- clips from nature documentaries.

One way of preparing for such videos is to watch the video and write short paragraphs, sentences, or instructions which describe the individual steps of the process. For example, the recipe below was written to match the visual narrative of Video 9.2, which is entitled *Fresh Guacamole by PES*.

IMAGE 9.3   *Still from the short film Fresh Guacamole by PES*

To make fresh guacamole

1 Take a ripe avocado, cut it in half and remove the stone.

2 Scoop out the green flesh with a spoon and put it in a bowl.

3 Peel an onion, dice it, and add it to the bowl.

4 Add a chopped tomato.

5 Add the juice of a lime.

6 Remove the seeds from a chilli pepper. Finely slice it and add it to the bowl.

7 Season the mixture with salt and pepper.

8 Mash all the ingredients together in the bowl.

9 Transfer the guacamole to a clean bowl and serve with chips for dipping.

Try this ☞ **Predict the verbs**

Tell students that they are going to read about a process (a method for making guacamole, for example). Before giving out the text, ask them to predict as many verbs as possible that they will see in the text or video.

Try this ☞ **Mystery ingredients**

Create a step-by-step description of a process. Turn it into a gap fill so that students have to guess or predict missing recipe ingredients, objects, materials, or verbs before they see the video. For example:

To make fresh guacamole

1 Take a ripe _____, cut it in half and remove the _____.
2 Scoop out the green flesh with a spoon and put it in a bowl.
3 Peel an _____, dice it and add it to the bowl.
4 Add a chopped _____.
5 Add the juice of a _____.
6 Remove the seeds from a _____. Finely slice it and add it to the bowl.
7 Season the mixture with _____ and _____.
8 Mash all the ingredients together in the bowl.
9 Transfer the guacamole to a clean bowl and serve with _____ for dipping.

Photocopiable © Oxford University Press

Try this ☞ **Over to the students**

Ask students to create illustrations or find online images for each of the individual steps in a process. Then ask them to prepare texts (spoken or written) in which they explain the process in their own words. In order to do this, they will have to make use of connective words and phrases such as:

First of all …   *The next thing that you have to do is …*
After that …   *Finally, …*

Students can then use movie editing applications or digital storytelling tools (see Appendix 7) to combine their words (onscreen or audio) and images. For an example, see Video 9.3.

Using video narratives

A standard way of using video in the language classroom is to pause it and ask students to guess what happens next. Film clips, short films, bloopers, **fail videos**, funny advertisements, and interesting caught-on-camera videos can all work well for this.

Prediction activities are naturally engaging, but require thought and planning. They can be divided into two categories: those in which language comes from the teacher and those in which language comes from the students.

Language from the teacher

These activities require more work on our part. The idea is to think of a number of outcomes for a video and present them to learners as a multiple choice. For example, in Video 9.4, five fearless teenagers carry out a fun experiment with an electric fence.

We could pause the video at 00:40 and ask students to guess which of the following is the actual outcome:

1 all of them get an electric shock

2 none of them gets an electric shock

3 only one of them gets electric shock.

In this particular case, the three sentences could be used to introduce determiners such as: *all*, *both*, *none*, *neither*, *any*, and *either*.

Try this ☞ **Multiple choice (from teacher)**

Show students a video and pause it before they see the outcome. Tell them that they have to guess what happens next and that you are going to give them a number of options. Drill each option before going around the class and nominating students at random to say which one they have chosen. In doing so, they will have to produce the target language.

Language from the students

After providing students with a model for language production they can make predictions of their own.

Try this ☞ **Multiple choice (from students)**

After demonstrating a multiple choice what-happens-next activity (see previous Try this suggestion) ask students to create their own. Students can then present their videos and ideas to the rest of the class. In order to do this, they should:

- Find a video in which something unusual or unexpected happens (you may want to put a time limit on the length of the video – 30 seconds, for example).
- Decide specifically when the video should be paused.
- Write three possible outcomes, one of which is the actual outcome.

This writing activity can be done in class if students have access to mobile devices and wireless internet. Alternatively, it can be done as homework.

Students can submit their ideas to you for correction before presenting them to their classmates either at the front of the class or, if they have access to mobile devices and internet connections, in groups or pairs.

Try this ☞ **Collaborative prediction**

Pause a video at a key moment, put students into small groups, and ask them to guess what happens next. Students in each group should reach a consensus decision about the outcome. This can encourage students to share and consider different ideas. Ask a spokesperson from each group to communicate their group's idea to the rest of the class before playing the whole video.

Try this ☞ **Little pieces of paper**

Give out little pieces of paper – one per student. Pause a video at a key moment, ask students to guess what happens next, and ask them to write down their ideas rather than shouting them out. Take back all the pieces of paper, read them out (this can be done anonymously) and correct errors before playing the video.

Try this ☞ **Hot and cold**

Pause a video at a key moment and ask students to guess what happens next. Give feedback by telling students how hot or cold their answer is (the hotter the guess, the closer it is to the correct answer). Invite students to rethink their ideas and continue to give feedback as they do. Examples of feedback language include:

- That's freezing. Can you make it hotter?
- That's getting (even) colder, I'm afraid!
- That's cool (which is better than cold).
- That's warm. You're getting there.
- That's getting hotter.
- That's very hot.
- That's boiling. You're so close!

As students call out their ideas, work with their language: reformulate their answers, offer corrections, praise good language, and write it on the board.

Try this ☞ **Multiple pause moments**

The prediction activities suggested above make use of short videos and single freeze frames. In some cases, longer videos with strong narratives can be paused at several key moments. At each moment, we can ask prediction questions which encourage students to interact with the video.

Language potential in prediction

Video prediction activities require creative thought. Students' ideas can be diverse and unpredictable, as can be the language that they use to express them.

However, when designing such activities, there are a number of factors that may influence or contribute to the specific grammar and lexis that we can teach or elicit.

1 Choice of video

The material which you select will have a bearing on the language that emerges in response to it. For example, if you choose a wedding-related video, students' predictions might require them to produce language which is related to that theme (*bride*, *groom*, *best man*, *bridesmaid*, etc.)

If we, the teachers, are providing the outcomes through multiple choice activities we can teach thematic lexical sets. For example, if you choose to use the sneezing baby panda video mentioned in Chapter 1, you could provide students with the following possible outcomes:

- Baby panda hiccups and mummy panda jumps.
- Baby panda yawns and mummy panda jumps.
- Baby panda coughs and mummy panda jumps.
- Baby panda sneezes and mummy panda jumps.
- Baby panda burps and mummy panda jumps.

2 Question

Once a video is paused, the most obvious question that we can ask is: *What happens next?* However, there are other possible questions, each of which can lead to the production of different language from students.

On page 50, we mentioned a stealth advert in which basketball player Kobe Bryant apparently jumps over a speeding car. In the moments leading up to the jump, the athlete prepares for the stunt as his friend tries to persuade him that it is a bad idea. In this case, a natural question to ask students would be: *What's he going to do?* The answers that they provide will involve a *going to* structure.

Other questions to consider include:

- **What happened next?** If we were using a historical piece of news footage, this question could be used to elicit past simple structures.
- **What does he/she say next?** This question can be used to invite students to speculate about verbal responses or replies from people in videos.
- **What would you do?** Ask this question when using videos which involve unexpected human behaviour. It can be used to introduce or elicit conditional structures.

3 Moment of pause

Sometimes, the specific moment that we choose to pause a video can affect the predictions that students make. For example, in the video mentioned above, it is better to pause the video before Kobe assumes a pre-jumping posture. If not, the answer to the question *What's he going to do?* will be too obvious.

Using video narratives

Creative writing

Short films, advertisements, or music videos with strong narratives can be good for creative writing tasks. The *Home Sweet Home* advertisement mentioned at the beginning of this chapter would be a good example. Rather than using the video to elicit quick predictions, ask students to complete a video narrative in any way that they like.

Try this ☞ **Complete the story**

Choose a video with a strong narrative. Show part of it to students and elicit or teach key language that they may need in order to write about it. Ask students to consider how the story ends and write down their idea. You may want to set a minimum number of words (perhaps 100) for the writing task.

Student-constructed narratives

By providing students with a list of key objects, people, and places that appear in a video, you can invite them to guess what happens in it. This can involve visualizing, collaborating, speaking, and writing.

Short videos with strong narratives work best for this. The following ingredients are central to a prank video. Can you guess what happens in it?

- two Japanese girls dressed-up as tourists
- two elderly Japanese men, also dressed-up as tourists
- several hidden video cameras
- an unsuspecting passer-by
- a van to create a distraction
- a camera

The video in question is Video 9.5.

Try this ☞ **Twenty questions**

On the board, write a list of items that are central to a video narrative. Tell students that they appear in a short video and invite them to guess what happens in it. Allow them to ask questions to which you can only answer yes or no. This will encourage students to make connections between the items, and construct a narrative.

Try this ☞ **Collaborative narratives**

Dictate a list of items that are central to a video narrative. For example, if you wanted to use the electric fence video (Video 9.4), you could select the following:

- five fearless teenagers (one with bare feet)
- four small plastic tables
- an electric fence
- a cameraman to film the experiment and put it on YouTube.

Put students into pairs or small groups and ask them to guess or predict what happens in the video. As they do this, circulate between groups, listen to ideas, and offer suggestions, clues, and feedback. Finally ask a spokesperson from each group to share their group's idea.

Using video narratives

↓ VIDEOTELLING

Videotelling refers to the everyday practice of communicating videos verbally. Imagine one person telling another about a piece of news footage, a funny advertisement, or a comedy sketch that the second person hasn't seen. Alternatively, imagine a conversation in which two people verbally deconstruct and analyse a scene from a film.

For the activities that are suggested below, short videos with strong narratives will work best.

Try this ☞ A video that you like

Ask students to choose a video that they like (one video per student). Perhaps you could set a theme – scenes from films, funny advertisements, or music videos, for example. Ask students to prepare a short presentation in which they tell the rest of the class about the video and explain what they like about it. After each presentation, the video can be shown to the class. Alternatively, this can be done as a writing task.

Try this ☞ A video that you dislike

Ask students to do the same as above but in this case, ask them to choose a video which they don't like (an annoying advertisement, for example).

Try this ☞ QR codes

Choose a number of short videos with strong narratives and create a QR code for each of them (see page 40). Print out the individual QR codes and distribute them to your students. You could do this randomly, or you could try to choose specific videos that you think will appeal to individuals. For homework, ask students to watch their video and prepare a description of it. The next day in class, ask them to mingle and tell each other about the videos that they were given. In each case, the listeners' task is to decide whether or not they are familiar with the video.

Try this ☞ Split viewing

Split the class into two: A students and B students. Show A students one half of a video while B students look away from the screen. Pause the video, ask students to change positions, and then play the video to the end. Repeat this process so that everyone in the class has seen their half of the video twice. Then put students into AB pairs and ask them to collaborate to construct the whole video narrative from start to finish. The *Home Sweet Home* advertisement (Video 9.1) is an example of a video that works well for this.

Try this ☞ Collaborative reconstruction

Some videos are designed to confuse. They require multiple viewings and lend themselves very well to collaborative analysis. An example of such a video is *Tick Tock*, a short film by Ien Chi which has a backwards narrative (Video 9.6). Ask students to watch the film as carefully as possible. Then ask students to get into pairs to verbally reconstruct the narrative before taking feedback.

Try this ☞ **Written words**

Students might prefer to describe videos through written words. There are online applications such as Metta.io (see Appendix 7) which allow users to combine other people's online videos and images, with their own onscreen text (see Video 9.7, for example).

Teacher-led videotelling

In the classroom, video narratives can be used as a basis for teacher-led, interactive storytelling sessions. Consider the following imaginary classroom dialogue in which a teacher tells his students about an online video.

> I want to tell you about a funny video that I saw on YouTube recently. It involves a mother and her baby. They are having a lazy day at home. Let's start with mummy – what do you think she is doing?
> [Teacher elicits ideas]

> In fact, she is sitting in the corner, eating a snack. What about baby? What do you think baby is doing?
> [Teacher elicits ideas]

> Well, baby is lying on the floor sleeping. I don't know where daddy is. Where do you think daddy is?
> [Teacher elicits ideas]

> So mummy is sitting in the corner eating a snack. And baby is lying on the floor sleeping. They both seem relaxed and happy. But then, suddenly, something unexpected happens. The unexpected thing wakes up baby and makes mummy jump.

> Can you guess what happens in the video? What is the unexpected thing that wakes up baby and makes mummy jump?

Why this works

In the activity above, a video narrative was relayed to a group of students by a human being rather than a computer screen. The video in question is Video 9.8. The process requires intensive listening and visualizing on the students' part. By visualizing, students construct a personalized mental representation of the video narrative being described.

Later, students can compare their visualizations with the actual video itself. When they do so, any language that they were unsure about during the videotelling becomes clear. In this way, meaning is resolved and students' experience of it is heightened.

Try this ☞ **Video hunt**

Describe a video to your students and then ask them to go online and find it for themselves. They will have to make use of their search skills for this. The activity works well if students have access to mobile devices and wireless internet in the classroom.

Try this ☞ **Preparing a videotelling text**

The key to a successful teacher-led videotelling session lies, in part, at the preparation stage. Choose a short video with a strong narrative and prepare a text which describes what happens. For example, the following text corresponds to Video 7.3 (*Blind Luck*).

> David is a creature of habit. He walks into the newspaper shop as he does every day. As he opens the door, a bell rings to let Matthew the shopkeeper know that a customer has come in.
> David walks towards the counter. As he does so, the men exchange just two words:
> 'Matthew?'
> 'David.'
> David puts his hand into his pocket, pulls out a coin and pushes it across the counter. Matthew picks it up and pushes back a scratch card.
> David pulls out another coin and scratches the card.
> £50,000!   £50,000!   £50,000!
> David tears up the scratch card and walks out of the shop.

Try this ☞ **Withholding information**

While preparing a videotelling text, consider information about the video that you can withhold from students. Questions can then be asked which get them thinking and collaborating. For example, try any of the following:

- Describe a video without telling students what genre it belongs to. Ask them to guess if the video is a cartoon, a short film, an advertisement, a music video, etc.
- Describe an advertisement without telling students what is being advertised. Ask them to guess the brand or product.
- Describe a video in part only. Ask students to guess what happens next.

You can also withhold essential information about the plot or the protagonists. In the text mentioned at the beginning of this section, we withheld the fact that the mother and baby are pandas. In the previous text we withheld the fact that the main character is blind. If you use the *Home Sweet Home* advertisement, you can withhold the fact that the protagonist is made of sugar lumps (see page 103). This can add an additional element of surprise to the activity.

Try this ☞ **Preparing for interactivity**

During a teacher-led videotelling activity, you can ask questions which involve students and encourage them to explore their visualizations. During the preparation stage, consider questions that can be used to drive the narrative. For *Blind Luck* (Video 7.3), we could ask:

- What do you think a creature of habit is?
- What do you think David buys every day?
- How many types of ticket can you think of?
- Where would you buy a lottery ticket/scratch card in your country/in the UK?
- Do you buy lottery tickets/scratch cards?
- Have you ever won?

- Why does the bell ring?
- Do David and Matthew know each other?
- Just two words pass between David and Matthew – what do you think the words are?
- What sort of relationship do you think they have?
- Can you guess how much David wins?
- How much is £50,000 in your currency?
- What would you do with £50,000?
- Why do you think David tears up the scratch card?

Try this ☞   Preparing notes

Prepare for a teacher-led videotelling session by preparing notes to use in the classroom. Your notes can include any or all of the following information:

- an outline of the story
- key language that you are going to use
- definitions of key words
- questions to ask students
- language you want to teach.

Notes can be written on cue cards, a single sheet of paper, a tablet computer screen, etc. Organize your notes using any format that you feel comfortable with (bullet points, a mind map, a flow diagram, etc.) Become familiar with your notes so that in class you can keep your eyes up and communicate with your students as much as possible.

Try this ☞   Storytelling gap fill

In a storytelling gap fill, the teacher selects a number of words or phrases from a narrative text and writes them on pieces of paper. These are then distributed to students who are asked to speculate what the story is about. The teacher then reads the text, pauses whenever he or she reaches one of the key phrases, and invites students to fill the gap with the correct phrase. Videotelling texts can work well for this type of activity. In the following example text, the isolated phrases are shown in bold:

> This is a story about the **sweetest little man you could ever meet**. One day, he wakes up in a very strange place: on top of a **picnic table in the countryside**. He looks around and realizes that **he has been left behind** by his family. He realizes that he has to get home **on his own**.
> He walks through a forest and then through a meadow. In the meadow, he sees an animal which scares him. It is a horse. He thinks that **it wants to eat him**. He runs away **as fast as he can**.
> He comes to a road and decides **to hitchhike**. Fortunately, a friendly lorry driver stops and gives him **a lift**. They have a nice conversation and stop for a coffee. But the lorry driver can see that the man is **homesick**.
> The lorry driver decides **to send him home**. When he gets home, he sees his family and then goes to bed.

Using video narratives

↓ GOING DEEPER

When we engage with a video, we get involved with it on many levels: we look for meaning and we interpret symbols; we notice details that contribute to the narrative or the emotion; we mentally connect the video to others that we have seen and contextualize it into our own world experiences; we form opinions about people in the video or the person behind the camera; we judge them, bond with them, and identify with them; we personalize and adopt experiences as if they were our own; we put ourselves into the picture and make predictions.

Importantly, the more we watch a video, the more we see in it. Students should be reminded of this when writing or speaking about video.

When speaking or writing about video, there is a lot to say. Words can be used to describe, recount, explain, analyse, criticize, and contextualize. When looking for things to speak or write about, students can be trained to look at any video from three different perspectives: the objective, the contextual, and the affective. These are shown in the following table which can be given out to students.

	We can speak or write about any of the following:
The objective (the video itself)	People in the video (their appearance, body language, relationships between them, etc.). Places (rooms, scenery, spatial relationships, etc.). Narratives (things that people do and things that happen). Spoken language (what is said, how it is said, accents, etc.). Non-verbal sounds (things we hear, sound effects, music). Information about genre (i.e. whether the video is a film clip, an advert, a viral video, a short film, etc.). Technical or aesthetic aspects (editing techniques, special effects, graphics, colour, etc.).
The contextual (the video and the world)	The title of the video. The video as an artifact: the story behind it. Information about who created the video. Information about where, when, how, and why it was created. Historical or cultural information that is necessary to appreciate the video. Technical information that is necessary to appreciate the video (film-making equipment and techniques). The video and reality (e.g. Has it been manipulated? Does it portray people and events fairly?) Discussion of stereotypes, ethics, symbolism, etc. Other materials or videos that the video is directly connected with.
The affective (the video and you, the viewer)	Thoughts, questions, or associations that come to mind as you watch the video. Relationships that you form/judgements that you make which relate to people in the video or behind the camera. Personal interpretations, speculation, opinion, analysis, or criticism. Personal memories or experiences that you recall as a result of the video. Other materials that you associate with the video as a result of your own experience (other videos, images, poems, films, etc.).

TABLE 9.1 *The three perpectives*

Photocopiable © Oxford University Press

Try this 👉 **Writing tasks**

Choose a video which introduces an issue – for example, a video which gives rise to questions such as:

- Do you agree that it is controversial?
- What is your opinion?
- What does it mean?
- How was it made? What techniques were used?
- Is it real or not?

Post the video in your virtual learning environment or similar online space along with your question(s). Ask students to write a composition in which they provide personalized answers. (You should set a minimum number of words.) As an alternative, ask students to choose their own videos based on a theme (video art, controversial adverts, stereotyping, propaganda, etc.).

Part 4   Video cameras in and out of the classroom

10

Privacy and permission

Different people have different attitudes to being filmed. While some may express enthusiasm or mere indifference to the idea, others may be overcome with terror at the very mention of a video camera. As teachers, we must be sensitive to people's feelings. It can be a bad idea to persuade reluctant subjects to stand for the camera.

As mentioned in Chapter 4, cultural sensitivities about what should or should not be filmed can further complicate things. It is essential to be aware of these.

Student autonomy

Importantly, the more autonomy a student has with a video-recording device, the less daunting the idea of being filmed becomes. Consider which of the following two situations would be less stressful to most people:

1 Two students act out a role-play in the classroom while the teacher films them with a video-recording device that belongs to the school. Later, the teacher plays the video for the whole class to see.

2 Two students plan and rehearse a role-play and then ask a classmate to film their performance when they are ready. The video-recording device belongs to one of the students being filmed. Later, the pair edit the video together and decide whether or not they are happy for it to be viewed by the whole class.

It is probably safe to assume that most people would prefer to have the control that the second situation offers.

↓ PERMISSION

Regardless of who your students are, if you want them to be seen or heard in videos, it is essential that you first obtain permission.

Adults

For groups of adults, verbal permission is generally sufficient if you wish to film them. Speak with your students and explain your intentions. Sometimes, the key to getting permission from adults is to convince them of the learning benefits that filming can bring. Make sure that you are ready to answer their questions.

If you have made videos with other groups, show them an example or two in order to demonstrate what you have in mind. However, in order to do this, you must get permission from the individuals who appear in the videos.

Another approach would be to write a friendly letter and distribute copies to each student. State your ideas, your suggestions, and your reasons for wanting to film them.

Be prepared for a mixed response. Some students will probably be more enthusiastic about it than others. And as mentioned before, don't force anyone who is unwilling to get involved.

If your adults agree to being filmed, give them advance warning about when the filming will happen. This will give them the opportunity to come to class looking their best.

Young learners and teenagers

For young learners and teenagers, permission from parents or guardians is essential. This will usually involve sending a letter home to be returned with a signature. It is important to state your reasons and specific intentions as accurately as possible.

Find out about your school's policy on filming students. Some schools ask parents to sign forms at the beginning of term or during enrolment to say that they are happy for their children to be filmed or photographed. Others may be less enthusiastic about the idea, and as teachers and employees, we have to comply with this.

 *Getting it right*

Writing a letter to parents

When composing a letter to your students' parents or guardians, you may want to explain or include the following:
- Your specific intentions: how you intend to incorporate video-recording devices into the child's learning
- Your reasons for doing so (motivation, to document progress, to encourage collaboration between students, etc.)
- What you intend to do with the video files (e.g. upload them and share them on the school virtual learning environment.)
- Whether or not you would like the parent or guardian to get involved. For example, you could invite them to monitor their child's videos and oversee the uploading procedure
- Information about the specific video-sharing site that you intend to use
- How you intend to deal with privacy issues
- Whether or not the child is expected to bring a video-recording device into class (a mobile phone, a tablet computer, a digital camera, etc.).

In order to illustrate your intentions as clearly as possible, you could also include a link to a sample video that was created by language learners. However, in order to do so, you must obtain permission from the students concerned.

↓ ONLINE DANGERS

Privacy and permission

Online bullying

An educational video created by the BBC tells the story of Janie, who, in an attempt to win tickets to see her favourite band, uploads a video of herself singing along to one of their songs. Unfortunately, some of Janie's spiteful classmates see the video and decide to tease and humiliate her about it on Facebook.

Unfortunately, Janie's story is quite unremarkable. It is the sort of thing that can and does happen. In 2011, the National Crime Prevention Council claimed that online bullying (often called cyberbullying) is a problem that affects almost half of all teenagers in the USA.

There are many questions that we have to ask:

- What is the nature of online bullying?
- How can we increase our awareness of it?
- How can we prevent it from happening?
- How can we train our students to deal with it? What support should we offer?
- How do we educate our students so that they are aware of the dangers and consequences?
- How should we collaborate with teachers and other parents to combat it?

There are many online resources that confront these issues. There are also videos which aim to educate young learners about responsibilities (see Appendix 8).

Online bullying is an issue for all teachers – not just those who make use of technology. It happens behind the teacher's back, beyond the classroom, and outside school hours. However, any teacher who intends to create video content in which students will appear should exercise particular caution: you don't want your own actions to make the situation worse.

Online hate

Unfortunately, the immediacy and anonymity of the internet, as well as its lack of editorial control, has made possible a rise in online hate. One common example is the internet troll – a person who intentionally disrupts online discussion groups through the use of deliberately provocative messages.

Online hatred is not, of course, limited to discussion groups. Virtually anyone who uploads blog posts or shares video content is at risk of encounters with unpleasant individuals whose purpose in life, it would seem, is to taunt and upset others.

In the world of online video, we have to be most careful about the comments sections on popular video-sharing sites such as YouTube.

↓ ONLINE SAFETY

Privacy and permission

1 Speak with your students

Students should be aware of the potential dangers associated with filming themselves. They should be aware that problems can arise internally within a group (especially for younger students and teenagers) or externally, from strangers online.

As mentioned before, there are many videos online that aim to educate young people on the dangers of bullying. It should be made absolutely clear that any form of bullying between classmates – either inside or outside school hours – will not be tolerated.

In the case of external bullying, students should be trained in how best to avoid it and how best to deal with it if it happens. For example, it is always a bad idea to engage in discussion with online haters – this is exactly what they want, and retaliation will often prolong things and worsen the situation.

2 Be aware of your school's policy

If your school has a policy regarding any of the issues mentioned in this chapter, it is essential that you are aware of it.

3 To upload or not to upload?

One way of avoiding online dangers is to take an offline approach. For example, if students were to film themselves with school video cameras and then hand them back to you, you remain the sole guardian of the resulting video files.

Alternatively, if students make use of their own devices, they will have to find a way to share their video files with you without uploading them onto a video-hosting site. For example, they could make use of email, cloud sharing, or memory sticks for this purpose (see page 36). Although these may be safer options, restricted accessibility can mean limited possibilities. Video tasks often work best when video files are freely available for everyone in the class to see.

4 Voice only options

In Chapter 8, we saw a video in which a Texan man introduced us to an armadillo that he caught in his yard (Video 8.1). While describing the animal, the only part of David that appeared in the video was his hands.

There are many possibilities for learning tasks that involve creating voice-only videos. We will discuss these in Chapter 11. The value of this is that when a student keeps out of the frame, there is more possibility for anonymity and less possibility for abuse.

Privacy and permission

5 Choosing a video-sharing site

The most practical way of sharing videos is by uploading them onto a video-sharing site, and a list of these is offered in Appendix 3.

Different video-sharing sites are associated with different online cultures. For example, Vimeo is often associated with quality user-generated content and independent film makers. SchoolTube is associated with learner-generated videos (especially young North American learners) and requires teacher moderation.

Video sites like these can be safer than more popular ones such as YouTube. Similarly, attitudes towards them can be more favourable.

6 Privacy settings

It is advisable to keep things as private as possible and this means investigating the various privacy options that a video-sharing site offers. On page 32 we saw that YouTube offers an unlisted option. This means that only people who have the video URL can watch it. Vimeo allows users to protect their videos with a password.

7 Comments

Teachers who wish to make use of popular video sites to share class content would be wise to disable the option for others to leave comments. If you want students to comment on each other's videos, one way of doing this would be to embed the videos on a blog, wiki page, or virtual learning environment, and ask students to leave comments directly on that page.

8 Involve parents

In Chapter 11, we will look at a number of ideas for video-making tasks and activities for students either in or out of the classroom. Although we are the ones who are responsible for setting these up, it is the students themselves who plan the videos, collaborate on them, create them with their own video-recording devices, and edit them. In this way, students become the owners of their own work.

If the task requires students to upload their work onto a video-sharing site, parents can get involved at this stage. Parents can monitor their children's work and make sure that they feel it is suitable for upload.

9 Don't let fear dictate

In 2006, New York teacher Gregg Breinberg started to upload performances of the elementary school choir, which he directed onto YouTube. The raw soulfulness and beauty of the children's performances caused many of the videos to go viral and as a result, the PS22 Chorus (from Public School 22 on Staten Island) is probably the best-known children's choir on the internet (see Video 10.1 for an example).

Imagine the excitement that the singers must have felt as they prepared for that video performance. And imagine how proud their parents must have felt when they saw their children singing from their hearts. And imagine how many other teachers must have been inspired by the video.

Now consider the number of people that Gregg must have persuaded in order to do what he did. If he or if any of the decision makers in his school had decided that it was too risky, then perhaps we would know nothing about the PS22 Chorus.

At best, creating and sharing videos which involve students can be very rewarding and have learning benefits. It would be a shame if we allowed fear to stop us at the first hurdle.

11 Cameras in the students' hands

↓ REASONS FOR FILMING

Both in and out of the classroom, video-recording devices in the hands of students can add depth and meaning to the activities, tasks, and projects that they do. Here are some reasons why:

Motivation

If students are aware that they are going to film a performance, there can be stronger reasons and enthusiasm to work on the preparation stages that lead up to it.

Documentation

Student-created videos can form an integral part of any language learner's portfolio. They can be revisited at later dates to monitor progress of their spoken language or just for fun.

Error correction

Error correction of spoken language has long presented teachers with a dilemma. Should we interrupt students to correct them immediately or should we wait until they have finished speaking? Option one is potentially distracting and can seem discourteous. On the other hand, if we wait too long, it is easy to lose the moment.

When we capture students speaking on camera, this is no longer a dilemma. Video can be paused and replayed. This allows us to elicit errors and corrections from students. It also allows us to draw attention to examples of good language so that students may learn from each other.

Time restrictions

Limited classroom time can mean that not everyone gets the opportunity to act out or read out their carefully-prepared role-plays, sketches, dialogues, stories, and poems.

If students are aware, from the beginning, that they are working towards the creation of a video product, the collaborative processes of writing, preparing, and rehearsing can be more meaningful. There will also be students for whom performing in front of a camera is less daunting than performing in front of the class.

Collaboration

Film-making activities are naturally and necessarily collaborative. With teacher guidance, a film-making task or project can create autonomy within a group of learners. The preparation process may involve scripting, rehearsing, choosing locations, planning shots, directing, and editing. All of this can be spread over any number of days.

An alternative medium

Recording spoken words on video can be regarded as an alternative to putting written words on paper. We can set up activities and tasks in which students are encouraged to use video-recording devices to capture their own stories, anecdotes, thoughts, opinions, and spoken compositions outside the classroom (This can be regarded as a **blended learning** approach.). **Webcams** can be particularly suitable for this.

An example is provided by Video 11.1, in which Jodie recounts a conversation that she had with a Chinese woman who was living in the UK and was married to a British man.

Sharing

We live in a noisy world. But the voice of the young person tends to cut through the rest. When children speak, people listen.

As English teachers, many of us are in a unique position. We have the potential to equip students with the language of international communication and manage video projects which will allow them to share their stories with the world.

↓ CONSIDERATIONS

Students' or teacher's hands?

For most students, video cameras in the hands of their peers will seem less intrusive than in the hands of their teacher. When filmed by classmates who are regarded as equals, most students will feel more relaxed and the result can be a better performance.

As teachers, we can set up activities, give clear instructions, and offer support where necessary. But by putting the technology in the students' hands, we give them total control of the technical and creative process.

When we concede control in this way, however, there are new questions that we should continually ask ourselves. For example:

- Are my students responsible enough to work with video cameras?
- Do they have the necessary technical abilities?
- Are they sufficiently motivated by the idea?
- Will everyone in a group benefit equally or will some students miss out on opportunities? For example, some students may be attracted to the job of holding the camera during filming, seeing it as an opportunity to avoid serious work.

Audio or video?

Many of the ideas that are suggested in this chapter involve the use of video-recording devices to record students' spoken English. In some cases, a voice recorder could be used instead.

Voice recorders are less obtrusive than video cameras. And for speaking activities that involve instant playback, they can be more practical. However, if we want students to document and revisit their work, it is much more engaging to experience the bigger picture and see how they looked, what they were wearing, where they were sitting, etc.

In addition, good communicators express themselves with their whole bodies, not just their spoken words. Sometimes, in order to understand a person's message, we have to be able to see them as well as hear them. For example, in Video 11.2, Ranin describes her favourite YouTube video. Notice how she makes use of gesture at 00:37 to communicate a central idea.

Gesture, facial expression, eye contact, posture, and other aspects of non-verbal communication contribute to meaning. We would miss all of this if we opted for audio only.

Equipment

In Chapter 1, we looked at a number of video-recording devices for classroom use. It was suggested that smart phones and tablet computers might be the most practical option as they are all-in-one tools. Students can use them to record, edit, and upload video without the need to transfer the file to another computer – a potentially inconvenient and time-consuming step.

Tripod or handheld?

There are a number of common mistakes that people make when they get behind a video camera. These include poor framing (see page 66), unnecessary panning (moving the camera from side to side), and unnecessary zooming. As a general rule, a camera should be locked on the subject and kept as still as possible. You may want to remind your students about this before asking them to film.

One solution is to use a tripod. There are many available for mobile phones and tablet computers that can bought relatively cheaply online.

Quiet spaces

The perfect classroom would be large and spacious. It would have lots of working areas – all sufficiently spaced apart – to allow groups of students to film without too much noise interference from each other. In the absence of such conditions, we may have to look for alternatives.

Try this ☞　**Other areas**

Look for empty rooms or quiet communal spaces in your school and find out if they could be used for filming during class time. After setting up a task or activity, send groups to these designated areas when they are ready to film.

Try this ☞　**A trip to the park**

Get permission to take a group of students to the park for filming. Groups can space themselves out sufficiently so that they can film in peace. By taking a central position yourself, you will be able to keep an eye on everyone. A school playground would be an alternative.

Locations

If a task or activity involves filming outside class time, remind students that a well-chosen filming location can enhance the impact of their work. As well as offering reduced noise levels, it can add aesthetic qualities to the picture and make the content of a video more relevant.

Ambitious teachers and students who wish to make the most of the classroom as a filming location might want to take inspiration from TV weather forecasters. These presenters are usually to be seen standing in front of large interactive maps but in reality, they are actually standing in front of a blue or green background.

Blue screens and **green screens** are easy to find online. They are generally not expensive and can be hung on your classroom wall. Many standard video editing applications have functions that will allow you to replace the green or blue background with an image of your choice (moving or non-moving). Look for the '**chroma key**', 'green screen' or 'blue screen' functions on your editor.

In fact, a 'green screen' or 'blue screen' is not always necessary. It can be perfectly adequate to film with a clean background – a white classroom wall, for example. There are free apps for mobile devices such as Touchcast (see Appendix 7) that make it easy for students to get creative and insert diverse backgrounds into their own videos.

Try this ☞　**Green screens**

By filming their own role plays or dialogues in front of a green or blue screen, students can later edit their video so that they are seen to be in virtually any location imaginable (on the moon, at the Antarctic, in a cartoon world, inside Buckingham Palace, etc.).

Costumes and props

Strategically-placed objects as well as the attire of those who appear in the picture can also contribute to a video in various ways. For example, if a student wanted to create a video in which they spoke about their favourite football team, they might want to appear in the picture wearing their team's strip or colours, or with a team poster in the background.

Product or process?

In many cases, a student-produced video will be the outcome of a collaborative process involving language use and planning (script writing, correction, learning the script off by heart, etc.). In other words, the video is a final product – something to work towards and something to show for the effort.

However, video can also be an integral part of a language-learning process. For example, we might want to use a camera to capture a sample of students' spoken English during a communicative speaking activity. Later, we could refer back to the video for error correction and feedback.

When using video-recording devices, we should be aware of our specific intentions and learning objectives. We should always ask ourselves how we want the video to fit into the bigger picture.

Providing video models

Before setting up tasks in which students produce videos of their own, it is important that they have an idea of the type of work that they are expected to produce. One of the best ways to communicate this is by showing them an example video which can serve as a model for their own.

Video models can be obtained from any of the following:

- **Online:** Look for video models online. For example, the video of Prince Charles reading the weather forecast (Video 7.2) would be perfect for setting up student-produced weather forecasts. Alternatively, whenever you make use of a video in class, consider whether it might serve as a model or source of inspiration for your students. For example, following an activity involving the baby armadillo video on page 93, students could create similar works of their own. For this, they would have to investigate a local animal or plant, and create a video in which they introduce it to the world.
- **Yourself:** Sometimes it is best to lead by example, which is exactly why I created Video 11.3.
- **Other teachers' students:** If you know any teachers whose students regularly make use of video-recording devices, the videos that they create might provide suitable models. Of course, you would need permission from the teacher and the students themselves if you wanted to show it to your own class (see Video 11.4), for example.

Try this ☞ **Helping students prepare**

When providing students with a video model for their own work, draw their attention to aspects of production as well as language. For example, ask them to think about the following:

- What type of camera do you think the speaker is using – a webcam, a mobile phone, a camcorder, etc.?
- Do you think that someone else is holding the camera or is it on a tripod?
- Do you think that the speaker prepared for the video? Do you think they decided what they were going to say and how they were going to say it?
- Do you think that the speaker is using notes?

Cameras in the students' hands

In or out of shot?

When privacy is a major concern, we may want to design video tasks in which students stay out of the frame. Later in the chapter, we will see some ideas.

Eyes on or off the camera?

When telling stories or presenting in front of a video-recording device, the speaker should decide whether to speak directly to the camera or indirectly to another person (the person holding the camera, for example). Option one is common for TV presenters and video bloggers. Option two is a common format for video interviewees.

Many people will prefer the second option: having a listener present can make the situation feel less awkward and more authentic. However, in many cases the first option will be the natural choice (speaking in front of a webcam when there is no one else around, for example).

When setting up such video tasks, raise students' awareness of these approaches and encourage them to choose the format that they are most comfortable with.

Try this 👉 **Compare the storytellers**

Find two videos – one to demonstrate each of the presenting approaches mentioned above. Show them to your students and point out the different ways of speaking in front of a camera before asking them to decide on their preference. Example videos include:

● Eyes on the camera: Video 11.5.
● Eyes on a person: Video 11.6.

Blending the classroom

The more students create video content either in or out of the classroom, the greater the need for a communal online space where they can organize, document, and share their work.

A virtual learning environment (VLE) would make this possible. Specifically, it would allow students to:

● Embed or link to videos that they create themselves and in doing so, submit their video assignments to you
● Upload any accompanying resources such as Word or PDF files (evaluations, transcripts, written compositions, etc.)
● Upload small video files directly onto the VLE and thus avoid the need for a video-sharing site
● Make their videos accessible to each other
● Leave comments on each others' videos directly on the VLE rather than on a video-sharing site such as YouTube.

Appendix 5 lists a number of specific virtual learning environments and other possibilities for this purpose.

Public or private viewing?

For students who have never watched themselves or their classmates speaking English on video, it can be quite a memorable experience for them to see themselves projected onto the big screen in the classroom. Among other things, whole-class viewing can be a good way for students to present their own videos to the rest of the class. It can also be a great opportunity for error correction and pointing out good use of language. Of course, you must get permission from students if you wish to show their videos in this way (see previous chapter).

Another possibility is to ask students to upload their own videos and share them on a virtual learning environment or other online space. Once they have done this, you can create tasks which involve students viewing and commenting on each others' work in their own time.

↓ SCRIPTS, NOTES, AND PROMPTS

Many of the suggested activities in this chapter require students to prepare what they are going to say before going in front of the camera. In some cases, this will involve writing out a full script. In other cases, it will involve semi-scripting and the use of prompts such as cue cards.

It is important that students know exactly what is expected from them with regard to preparation and execution. Here are three possible approaches:

1 Students learn a script by heart

Activities which promote memorization of language are extremely valuable for language acquisition. Learning a script by heart before performing it in front of a camera is an everyday process for actors, and an excellent activity for the language classroom. Encourage students to rehearse together and help each other commit their lines to memory.

Try this ☞ **Creating and acting out a dialogue**

Put students into pairs and ask them to work together to write out a dialogue for a given situation. Examples could include:

- Making an excuse to avoid doing something you don't want to do
- Meeting a long-lost friend by chance in the street
- Reporting a petty crime to a police officer
- Making a complaint in a restaurant
- Interviewing the worst job applicant in the world
- Confessing a dark secret to your oldest friend
- Explaining directions to a taxi driver
- Making small talk with a hairdresser.

Take in all dialogues for correction and give them back the next day. Students should then learn the corrected versions by heart and perform them in front of the camera.

Cameras in the students' hands

2 Students make use of a teleprompter

A teleprompter is a device which allows presenters and reporters to read a script, word-for-word, without taking their eyes off the camera.

There are many teleprompter programs and apps available for laptop and tablet computers (see Appendix 7). By pasting a text into the app and clicking 'play', students can create a scrolling script which should be placed as close to the camera lens as possible. This can be useful for presentations or storytelling activities.

IMAGE 11.1   *A classroom camera with tablet teleprompter*

Reading from a teleprompter is a skill that can be fun to experiment with in the classroom. Teleprompter apps allow users to change font size and scrolling speed and it is important for students to get the correct combination. Font size should be big enough to allow them to read the script from where they are positioned. Scroll speed should be slow enough to allow them to keep up with the script.

Try this ☞   **News report**

Put students into news teams and tell them that they have to work fast to produce a TV report for a hot story of the day. Give out a selection of silly or fictitious headlines such as *Motorist dressed as Batman escapes ticket* or *Woman attacks man with bowl of spaghetti* (there are a lot of these to find online by typing 'funny news headlines' into a search engine). Ask students to prepare a script for any or all of the following:

• An in-studio presenter (or a male and female presenter team)
• An on-the-scene reporter
• A statement from an eyewitness.

After you have seen the scripts and offered language suggestions and corrections, ask students to write their corrected versions into a teleprompter application on a laptop or a mobile device (see Appendix 7). Let them practice reading before filming. Note that there are also apps that allow students to add news-report style graphics to the screen (see Appendix 7).

3 Students make use of notes or prompts

If students are required to plan an outline of what they are going to say as opposed to writing a word-for-word script, they may want to make use of notes or prompts. Individuals have their own preferred formats – cue cards, mind maps, bullet points – and you can discuss possibilities with your students.

Most importantly, when speaking in front of a camera, students should not become overly-dependent on their notes. The idea is not to create a video of a person reading a text! Presenting requires eyes-up communication and this means looking directly at the camera or audience as much as possible.

↓ COLLABORATIVE VIDEO ACTIVITIES

The ideas that are suggested here involve students from the same class working together either in or out of the classroom.

Capturing samples of spoken interaction

Video cameras can be used in the classroom to capture dialogues between students.

Try this ☞ Trios

On page 69, we saw a speaking activity in which students discuss a list of 'would you rather' questions. For an activity like this, try putting students into trios instead of pairs. The third student's job is to hold the video camera and film the discussion between the other two. Video-recording devices have timer displays so the camera person can have the additional role of ensuring that speakers speak for a minimum amount of time (ninety seconds, for example). After each discussion, the camera should be passed on so that roles can change.

Try this ☞ Group discussion

When students are required to speak in larger groups, group members can nominate a camera person to film their interaction. The camera person can stay out of the discussion but should have the following secondary roles:

● To make sure that everyone speaks English and not their mother tongue
● To make sure that everyone contributes to the discussion.

Try this ☞ Observing interaction

Any video involving spoken interaction between students can be revisited for reflexion or feedback. For example, ask students to watch their videos and pay attention to the ways in which they interact. In particular, ask them to consider:

● How much did you listen to each other?
● How much did you respond to each other's ideas?

This can be useful for speaking exam preparation, especially if students are able to compare their video with a similar one involving expert speakers of English, such as the one between Jess and James (Video 5.5).

Goal-orientated speaking tasks

Video cameras can be used to capture the end product of a collaborative speaking task. For example, in Video 11.7, Ruben shares his group's theory about what happens in Video 9.5 during a collaborative narratives activity (see Try this activity on page 111).

Try this ☞ Spokesperson

In Part 3, we saw a number of Try this activities where students work together to reconstruct, predict, or hypothesize about video narratives. See for example:

- Collaborative storybuilding on page 80
- Collaborative prediction on page 109
- Collaborative narratives on page 111
- Collaborative reconstruction on page 112.

In such cases, groups can nominate a spokesperson to communicate their consensus idea to the camera. The process can work as follows.

1 Group members share ideas and reach a consensus.
2 The group nominates a spokesperson.
3 The spokesperson rehearses what he or she is going to say to the camera. Meanwhile, other group members listen and provide content or language feedback.
4 Someone in the group films the spokesperson's answer.

Try this ☞ Big screen viewing

Following an activity like the one that we have just seen, play each group's video on the projector for the rest of the class to see. Encourage students to comment on other groups' ideas. If groups have similar ideas, compare the language choices they made to express them.

Try this ☞ Spot the liar

Put students into small groups and ask them to share personal stories or anecdotes. Help to get them started by telling them one of your own or suggesting themes such as:

- An embarrassing incident
- A time when you lied and got caught out
- A time that you cheated and got away with it (i.e. you didn't get caught)
- An amazing coincidence that you experienced
- A time when you got into trouble at school
- A time when you won a prize
- A time when you lost or found something very valuable
- Your claim to fame.

Ask students to choose the best story that they have heard in their group. Once they have done this, each group member should prepare to tell that story in front of a video camera as if it is their own (without using any notes!). After filming, students can share their videos online. For homework, students can watch each others' videos and attempt to work out who is telling the truth and who is lying. The group who fools the most people wins. Note that for this activity to work, groups should be out of sight and out of earshot of each other during preparation.

Capturing group performances

By group performances, we could be referring to any of the following:

- Prepared or improvised dialogues, role-plays, or interviews
- Acted-out scripts or recreated film scenes
- Student-produced documentaries and video projects
- Student-produced adverts, news reports, and weather reports.

Try this ☞ **Directors**

For a dialogue activity such as the one described on page 132, put students into trios rather than pairs. All three students should collaborate on the scriptwriting. But whereas two of the students have acting roles, the third student is the director. It is the director's job to do the following:

- Offer feedback to the actors during their rehearsal and test them to make sure that they know their lines by heart
- Choose a filming location
- Set up the scene (arrange furniture and props, etc.)
- Make equipment decisions (camera, handheld, tripod, etc.)
- Manage the actors (tell them where they should be standing or sitting, etc.)
- Plan frames, angles, and shots.
- Shoot!

If necessary, all students can work together on the editing process.

Try this ☞ **Adding English subtitles**

Students can role play or act out a dialogue in their own language. After filming, they can translate their words into English and add English subtitles to the video.

Try this ☞ **Film-making competition**

Put students into groups and ask them to collaborate outside class to create a video in which they do any of the following:

- Bring a script to life
- Choose a speaking scene from a film that they like, watch it carefully and recreate it themselves. A video model is provided by Video 11.8.
- Create a 'televised' production of a short story from a graded reader
- Create a documentary about a local person, place, or curiosity.

Once groups have completed their work, have a class viewing session and take votes for the best production. If possible, get outsiders involved in the viewing and voting process. If a group chose to recreate a scene from a film, the rest of the class can guess what the film is.

↓ SPOKEN COMPOSITIONS

Recording spoken words on video can be regarded as an alternative to putting written words to paper. Student access to video-recording devices allows us to set up monologic speaking tasks, either in or out of the classroom. Students could do any of the following:

• Create a one-minute summary or review of a book, film, or computer game
• Describe how to prepare a simple recipe
• Read a poem or text out aloud
• Share a personal idea or opinion (how they would change the world, what makes them angry, the place in the world that they would most like to visit and why, etc.).

Note that although these are non-collaborative activities, students may wish to seek the help or involvement of a friend or parent in some cases (to hold the camera, for example).

Try this ☞ **Personal stories**

In class, share a personal story with your students. You could choose from any of the following example themes:

• A particularly memorable food experience
• The most exciting sporting moment that you ever witnessed (either live in person or on TV)
• Your earliest memory
• An unforgettable journey
• The worst accident you have ever had.

For homework, ask students to create videos in which they do the same. These can be shared on a virtual learning environment.

Try this ☞ **Giving students a choice**

Not everyone likes the idea of filming themselves. Allow students to decide whether they want to complete a homework task as a written composition or by speaking on video.

Try this ☞ **True and false introductions**

At the beginning of a course, ask students to create and share short videos in which they introduce themselves. Ask them to include some interesting facts about themselves but to include one piece of false information. Later, ask students to watch each other's videos, attempt to identify the false piece of information, and leave their answer in a comment. This would work particularly well for blended or online courses.

Try this ☞ **Commentary-only videos**

There are many possible video tasks that lend themselves to commentary-only formats. By pointing the video camera at a subject, students can stay out of the picture but record their spoken words on the audio. This may be desirable for shy students or in situations when privacy is an issue. Note that commentary can be added either during, or after the filming. In the case of the latter, students would

Cameras in the students' hands

have to record the commentary on an audio device (a smartphone, for example) and use a video editor to synchronize the tracks. Here are some example tasks students could carry out:

- Create an instructional video. Someone else holds the camera and makes sure that only the student's hands appear in the frame. A video model is provided by Video 11.9.
- Give a video tour of their home and describe the various rooms and what they are used for. Students could simultaneously hold the video-recording device and provide commentary, so that they can be heard but not seen.
- Demonstrate a recipe and give instructions as they do so. Someone else holds the camera and makes sure that only the student's hands appear in the frame. Alternatively, students film a friend or parent in the kitchen and provide commentary as they do so.

Try this ☞ Pets

Consider possibilities for videos which involve students' pets or those of friends, relatives, or neighbours. Students could do any of the following as a commentary-only video:

- Introduce a pet and describe it. A video model is provided by Video 11.10.
- Tell a story about a pet or talk about an unusual or interesting aspect of its behaviour. A video model is provided by Video 11.11.
- Give their pet a voice. A video model is provided by Video 11.12.

Try this ☞ Videos from a school trip

A school trip can provide opportunities for video tasks. If a museum or gallery is happy for students to use video cameras (you will have to find out beforehand) set up tasks in which students present an exhibit to the camera. They can mention any or all of the following: its title; its location in the venue; the story behind it; the history behind it; why they like it; what they would do with it if they were allowed to take it home; six questions that they would like answered about it; ten adjectives that they would use to describe it. Students could present the objects while speaking to the camera, or this could be done as a commentary-only video.

↓ QUESTIONS AND ANSWERS

Video-recording devices can be used to set up question-and-answer sessions between students and other parties.

Try this ☞ Video exchanges

Social networking sites have made it easy for teachers in far off places to make contact and collaborate on projects. An example project would be one in which two groups of students exchange video questions and answers about each other's lives and culture. An example of such a project can be seen at www.schoolexchange.wikispaces.com.

Try this ☞ **Cultural curiosities**

For any group that is taking a course away from home (in an ESOL context, for example), ask each student to create and share a video in which they do the following:

- Comment on an aspect of life or culture which relates to their new environment – an observation about something that they find interesting or unusual, and why it is different from what they are used to.
- End the video with a question which relates to their observation. Sample question: Video 11.13.

Post students' video questions on a communal space such as Glogster, Padlet, or Pinterest (see Appendix 5) and share the link with anyone who is familiar with your students' new environment (friends, families, other teachers, other students, etc.) Invite recipients to choose a question and create a personalized video response which they can then upload and add to the space. Video 11.14 provides a sample answer.

✓ *Getting it right*   **Making things easy for yourself**

A project like this will take a substantial amount of work on the teacher's part. Inevitably, you will have to pick up a video camera yourself and go looking for responses to unanswered questions. For this reason, you should avoid using the format with large groups.

↓ EVALUATION OF STUDENTS' WORK

If students are expected to create and deliver video assignments, we need a system for feedback, evaluation, and assessment. One possibility is to make use of a scoring rubric designed for students to evaluate their own work.

The example scoring rubric on page 140 has been designed specifically for video tasks in which students present directly to a camera. Different video tasks would require different combinations of criteria. For example, if we were evaluating videos of student discussions, we would need to include criteria which draw attention to aspects of their interaction.

Try this ☞ **Self-evaluation**

As part of a video assignment, ask students to submit a completed scoring rubric along with their video. As the teacher, you can then provide feedback on students' videos and also feedback on their own evaluations. By self-evaluating with scoring rubrics in this way, students can broaden their awareness of what good communication requires, and identify areas for their own development.

Try this ☞ **Peer evaluation**

Instead of evaluating their own videos, students can use scoring rubrics to evaluate each others' work. Assign each student a partner for this purpose. With access to each others' videos outside the classroom, students can watch and evaluate them at home by filling in scoring rubrics. Back in the classroom, students can be paired up for face-to-face feedback.

Cameras in the students' hands

Cameras in the students' hands

Self-evaluation scoring rubric

Watch your video and rate your own performance. For each of the following, give yourself a mark between 1–4:

1 = could be a lot better   **2** = not bad   **3** = pretty good   **4** = very good

Criterion	Things to consider	Mark and comments
Overall	• How well do you communicate? Is it easy for the listener to understand you? • Do you put your ideas in a logical order? • Are you concise or do you speak more than necessary?	
Clarity	• How clear is your spoken English? • Does the volume and speed at which you talk affect communication?	
Fluency	• Does your spoken English flow naturally or do you have to stop to think about how to say things in English?	
Markers, connectors, and fillers	• Successful communicators use high-frequency phrases such as: *so anyway, in other words, I would say that, you know what I mean?* Do you?	

Pronunciation	• Can you identify any individual words or phrases that you pronounce incorrectly? Pay attention to:
	  – the individual vowel and consonant sounds that you produce
	  – the number of syllables that individual words should contain
	  – word and phrase stress.	

Phrasing and intonation	• Phrasing and intonation can be thought of as vocal punctuation. Listen to an online presentation (a TED talk, for example) and pay attention to how and when the speaker's voice rises, falls, and pauses. How does it compare with yours?	
Vocabulary	• Do you use a good range of vocabulary when you are speaking? Do you make good choices of words and phrases? • How often do you have to use your own language or paraphrase when you don't know a word in English?	
Grammar	• How accurate is your grammar? Do you spend too much time thinking about it and forget to concentrate on other aspects of spoken English? Remember that transcribed spoken language can naturally look quite untidy on paper.	
Presenting in front of a camera	• Do you keep good eye contact and posture? Or do you look down and appear nervous? • If you are using notes, is it obvious that you are doing so?	
Technical aspects	• Is the camera still or is it a bit shaky? If someone held it for you, did they move it unnecessarily? • How well is your shot framed? Do you fill the screen or are you standing too far away from the camera? If you are standing far from the camera, does the audio suffer as a result? • Did you edit your video to remove any unnecessary parts?	

TABLE 11.1   *A scoring rubric for student self-evaluation*

Photocopiable © Oxford University Press

Try this ☞ **Transcripts**

When focusing on the details of spoken language (grammar and vocabulary, for example) a transcribed text can be easier to work with than a video. Once students have captured a sample of their spoken English on video, ask them to transcribe an excerpt from it (approximately 250 words). Ask students to do any of the following:

- Identify the most recently-learned word, phrase, or structure that they use
- Identify words, phrases, or structures that they overuse
- Consider whether or not their language choices could have been improved
- Evaluate their grammatical accuracy
- Identify any consistent errors that they make.

Note that it is important that students are aware of the fact that transcribed spoken language naturally looks messy and does not necessarily imply bad communication. Also, even native English speakers make mistakes! Introduce students to this idea, using a transcribed spoken text (see the baby armadillo video referred to on page 93, for example).

Try this ☞ **Synchronized notes**

Videonot.es is an online application that allows users to write onscreen notes that refer to specific time moments of a video (see Appendix 7). Notes are then saved online and synchronized with the video so that later, a user can click on any note and the video will skip directly to the moment at which it was written. Tools like this can be useful for students to add evaluative comments to their own videos and share them with their teacher or other students. Similarly, teachers can use such tools to provide feedback.

↓ NON-CAMERA VIDEO POSSIBILITIES

There are possibilities for creating online videos which do not involve the use of video-recording devices.

Animated movie generators

There are a number of animated movie generators that have proved to be very popular with language teachers. Appendix 7 offers a list of these. These can be used to animate short exchanges and conversations between characters.

Try this ☞ **Animated videos**

As an alternative to classroom role-play or dialogue activities, ask students to use an animated movie generator to create and share their own animated exchanges between cartoon characters. The theme could be making an excuse, confessing a secret, or giving directions (see the Try this suggestion on page 132 for more ideas). Students could then watch each other's animations and vote for the best ones.

Cameras in the students' hands

Digital storytelling and video remix tools

There are a number of apps and applications which allow students to create multimedia montage videos which include images, drawings, video clips (their own or other people's), onscreen text, and audio. Some of these are listed in Appendix 7.

Student drawings

By making scans of students' drawings, you can import the resulting images into a film-editing or digital storytelling application (see above), intersperse it with text, and add audio. We already saw an example of this on page 97. Below are two more ideas.

Try this ☞ **Illustrate a song**

Set up activities in which students illustrate song lyrics. You can then scan their work and create an unofficial fan video. Video 11.15 provides a model.

Try this ☞ **Student-generated flash cards**

Ask students to create simple drawings of a given situation (a man or woman buying flowers, a chicken crossing the road, etc.) Ask each student to think of a reason why the situation is happening and write it on the back of their drawing. Later, correct your students' texts, scan their drawings, and create an image–text video montage. Video 11.16 and Video 11.17 provide models.

12 Cameras in the teacher's hands

There are times when it can be practical for the teacher to be in control of the video camera. Here are some situations:

Extrovert students

In many cases, it would be unfair to single out an individual student and ask them to speak in front of a video camera. However, in any group, there may be one or two extroverts who would be happy to do so.

Extrovert students are the ones who seem completely at ease speaking English in front of the rest of the class. They are the ones who often share funny stories and make others laugh. Sometimes they dominate discussion and we worry that they deny shyer students the opportunity to contribute. But sometimes they can be an asset, especially if they have a higher level of English than the rest of their group.

We can take advantage of extrovert students by capturing their spoken texts on video and using them for whole-class language study activities. If you know a group well, let your own judgement tell you whether or not it would be appropriate to ask an individual to speak in front of the camera. Make sure you are explicit in your reasons for doing so, and most importantly, don't force anyone to do something that they don't want to do.

Try this ☞ **Make an excuse**

If an extrovert student arrives late to class, tell them that you will forgive them on one condition: that they can provide you with an excellent excuse (it doesn't have to be true) and let you film them as they do so. Later, play the video on the projector and use it for an opportunity to draw attention to good language and/ or elicit suggestions for corrections.

Try this ☞ **Suspect interrogation**

Write a series of 'have you ever' questions on the board such as:

- Have you ever been arrested?
- Have you ever done a runner from a restaurant?
- Have you ever appeared on TV?
- Have you ever milked a cow?
- Have you ever dyed your hair a crazy colour?

Ask for a volunteer extrovert student to sit on a chair at the front of the classroom – the interrogation chair. Then ask the rest of the class to decide which question they are going to ask the suspect. Whatever the question, the suspect has to answer 'yes' and then tell the story as elaborately as possible. Naturally, this has to be captured on film for police records! After some interrogation by student police officers, everyone should decide whether the suspect is lying or telling the truth. Before the suspect reveals whether the story is true or not, play the video on the projector and draw attention to good language and/or elicit suggestions for corrections. It is also fun to look for signs that suggest that the suspect is lying (eye contact, touching nose, hesitations, etc.).

Whole-class videos

With a video camera in hand, we can record classroom activities, games, and performances which involve the whole group.

Try this ☞ **Songs and chants**

On page 124, we saw a video of the PS22 Chorus, an elementary school choir from New York. From the front of the room, their teacher captured their performance by moving the camera around from student to student. This is a useful technique for filming songs, chants, drills, and other recitals. Later, you can share the video with students and parents on a class blog, Facebook page, or VLE.

Try this ☞ **Demonstrating an activity**

Sometimes, a language learning game or activity may seem to work well with one class but not with another. This may come down to unclear instructions on our part. Alternatively, it could be the case that a group of students just can't 'see' what it is that they are expected to do. In such a situation, try filming a group of students successfully engaged in the activity so that you can show the video to another class and demonstrate by showing rather than telling.

Try this ☞ **Word of the day**

Five minutes from the end of a class, ask everyone to choose their favourite new word, phrase, or collocation from that day's lesson. When everyone has made their decision, start filming. Move the camera around the class from student to student, and ask everyone to tell you which piece of language they have chosen, and also why they like it. Start the next day by playing the video on the projector and thus revise the previous day's language.

Try this ☞ **Doubling a picture**

Doubling is a technique from the world of psychodrama and can be a great way of setting up a whole-class dialogue in the classroom – an event that can be worth capturing on camera. Start with a thought-provoking picture on the projector which features people or animals (the protagonists). Ask students to each write three questions that they would put to the protagonists if they could meet them (in this activity animals can talk!). You will now need volunteer students to sit underneath the picture – one student to represent each protagonist. Invite the rest of the class to ask their questions to the protagonists in the picture. The students sitting underneath the picture answer on the protagonists' behalf. After some initial moments of awkwardness, this activity can quickly develop momentum as students start improvising questions and answers. Meanwhile, your role can be to film the event for later language feedback with, for example, a focus on question forms.

In the classroom, there are situations where putting ourselves in front of the camera can benefit our students, our peers, or ourselves. Importantly, when a camera is pointed at the teacher, the resulting video may also capture interaction with students. Examples are provided by Video 12.1 and Video 12.2.

Camera issues

It is notoriously difficult to generate good video footage of whole-class interactions. A professional production company would make use of multiple manned cameras and professional audio recording equipment for the job. In an amateur context, a single recording device pointed at the teacher is probably the most practical option.

As mentioned earlier, a camera can be either mounted on a tripod or handheld. If mounted on a tripod, you will have to consider carefully where to position it. This will depend on the size and layout of your classroom. For the handheld option, you will have to choose a camera person for the job – a responsible student or an observer, for example.

As we see below, there are advantages and disadvantages associated with both of these approaches.

	Advantages	Disadvantages
Tripod option		
Note that Video 12.1 was created in this way. Since it was filmed in a very small classroom, the audio is fairly clear. But note the shaky floor!	This can be the least disruptive and unobtrusive option. After setting up a camera at the back of the classroom, for example, you can leave it there and forget about it. With this option, you can record a whole lesson.	Usually, the closer the camera is to the teacher, the more obtrusive it will be. But if it is too far away, the audio will be unclear and the video will be useless. Be very careful – cameras on tripods can easily be knocked over by students and (unexpected) visitors! It is vital to compose the shot so that you are well framed. It is very easy to create videos in which your head is missing! When composing the shot, ask a volunteer to sit or stand where you are going to be. If you walk around the classroom, you will leave the frame and be out of the video. Floors can be unstable and tripods can shake.

	Advantages	Disadvantages
Handheld option Note that Video 12.2 was created in this way. A student volunteer held the video camera and followed me as I moved around the room.	This is the natural option for mobile devices. The individual with the camera can frame the shot and follow you around the room as you move. The camera can be brought closer to you and audio quality will be better.	This only works for filming short periods of time. It would be unfair and/or disruptive to expect students to be tied to the camera for long periods. A naughty student with a video camera can be a recipe for disaster. Choose your camera person wisely!

TABLE 12.1   *Advantages and disadvantages of tripod vs. handheld camera options*

Privacy issues

As the guardians of videos like these, we may want to share them with our students or with our peers.

However, many of the privacy issues discussed in Chapter 10 can also apply to teachers. For this reason, use your own judgement to decide how available you choose to make your videos.

There is an additional issue here with regard to comments from students that may be inadvertently caught on camera.

Imagine, the following situation, for example: You set up a camera at the back of the classroom to film the day's lesson. As is often the case, everyone in the class forgets it's there. Half way through the lesson, two students exchange private remarks that are picked up by the audio – remarks that were never intended to go public. This could result in a very embarrassing situation for a lot of people and it is essential to know how to deal with it.

The best solution is to speak to your students. Remind them that there is a camera in the classroom that could pick up unintended comments, especially from those sitting close to it. Implement a 'delete without questions' policy. That means that any student can approach you, in private, at the end of the class and ask you to delete the video without specifying their reasons for doing so.

Capturing teacher texts

The most important source of language input for any learner must surely be that which comes from their teacher. Any activity in which we make use of our own voice for this reason can be enhanced with a video-recording device.

Try this ☞   **Filming instructions**

Video cameras are perfect for capturing teacher instructions and then allowing students to hear them, word-for-word a second or third time. This may strengthen student comprehension of the instructions and also increase the chance of them noticing grammatical and lexical aspects of the language. This technique is illustrated in Video 12.3.

Later, by transcribing our own words, we can create language learning activities which draw attention to aspects of the language. For example, after completing the following gap-fill activity, students can watch the original video of their teacher and thus correct their answers.

I want _____ _____ _____ a picture of a visitor in the Field Museum of Natural History in Chicago. The visitor is standing _____ _____ _____-hand side of the picture in the foreground. The visitor is speaking with a guide, who is standing _____ _____ _____-hand side of the picture in the foreground. The visitor is _____ _____ Sue, the _____ and _____ _____ T. rex skeleton _____ discovered. Sue is in the _____ of the picture _____ left. There are two _____ _____: one _____ out of the visitor's mouth and another _____ out of the guide's mouth.

Try this ☞ **Filming with a hidden camera**

If you have a particularly good relationship with a group of students, there are fun possibilities for hiding a video camera in the classroom and filming an exchange without their knowledge. In <u>Video 12.4</u>, students were the subject of a prank with a teaching objective.

The next day, students watched the video and heard the story a second time. Meanwhile, the teacher paused the video and drew attention to useful language, which was written on the board.

Dictogloss

A dictogloss is a versatile activity with a basic two-step format:

1 Students hear a text

The text in question can be a short story or anecdote which you usually read aloud two or three times. From the students' point of view, this requires the following:

- Intensive listening
- Identifying the central ideas and key language (names, words, phrases, collocations, structures, etc.).

2 Students reconstruct the text

Importantly, the reconstruction is not a word-for-word reassembly of the text (that would be impossible). The idea is for students to capture the meaning of the text and rewrite it as accurately as possible, using their own words whenever necessary. This involves:

- Putting the central ideas and key language into the correct chronological order
- Gluing them together with good grammar, discourse, and punctuation.

To this basic format, there are dozens of possible variations. Here are a few:

- We can provide students with key words and phrases from the text before they hear it. We can then ask them to predict what the text is about. (Note that this is similar to the Storytelling Gap Fill idea on page 115).

- After hearing the text, we can support students by providing them with some key language to incorporate into their reconstructed texts.
- Students can make notes as they listen to the text. They can write down the central ideas and key language that they hear.
- Students can reconstruct the text collaboratively in groups or pairs.
- Students can share and compare their reconstructed texts and make changes if they wish to do so.

Try this ☞ **Capturing a story on video**

Tell your students a short story or anecdote and film yourself as you do so. Tell the story naturally as if you were speaking to a friend. Although you may decide to prepare and practise beforehand, it should not appear to be scripted. Once students have heard the story, ask them to write it as accurately as possible from memory. Before they do so, let them watch the video so that they can experience it again, a second or third time. An example of this is provided in Video 12.5.

Why this works

Stories, jokes, and anecdotes are often communicated better if they are not fully scripted. The problem is, however, that an unscripted story cannot be told the same way twice, and this is a requisite for a dictogloss activity. Video cameras solve this problem. We can use them to capture and replay spoken texts, and then refer back to the video to find out how we specifically expressed an idea or part of the narrative.

Try this ☞ **Telling a joke**

When teaching in a one-to-one situation, tell your student a joke and ask them to film you as you do so. Let your student watch the video and hear the joke a second – or even a third – time. Then change roles – as your student retells the joke in their own words, you film their performance. Later your student can transcribe both videos and compare the language in the transcripts. This can be an excellent way for students to learn new ways of expressing ideas in their target language.

– Sample teacher video: Video 12.6.
– Sample student video: Video 12.7.

Try this ☞ **Emergent language**

The previous Try this idea can be reversed: a student tells you a story or anecdote and repeats it for the video camera. Then ask your student to film you telling the same story or anecdote from memory (you can recount it either in the first or second person). After transcribing both versions, students can compare the facts and the language.

Video chat applications

Applications such as Skype, Facetime, Google Hangouts, and ooVoo are familiar to many of us (see Appendix 7). With an online connection and a webcam, they can be used to bring virtual visitors into the classroom.

Try this ☞ **Inviting a virtual guest into the classroom**

Use a video chat tool to bring a friend or family member into the classroom. This could be any of the following:

- Someone to be interviewed by your students (a friend with an interesting job, for example)
- A friend that you refer to a lot in class – someone that you would like your students to meet in person
- A family member with an interesting story to tell.

Before class, arrange a specific time for the video call and make sure that you let the person know your intentions. In class, project the video image onto a screen for everyone to see, amplify the audio, and point your webcam towards your students so that the guest can see who they are talking with.

↓ THE FLIPPED CLASSROOM

If you ever studied maths, technology, or science at school, the chances are that you will remember your teacher standing at the front of the classroom, explaining principles and clarifying concepts. Homework would probably have consisted of reading and problem solving.

In some blended learning contexts (especially those involving content-based subjects like maths, technology, or science) this process has been reversed or 'flipped' to some extent. In a **flipped classroom**, students watch lectures at home and dedicate classroom time to putting theory into practice.

Part of the idea is that the teacher creates or sources interactive video presentations and shares them with students online. In their own time, students can then watch them, process them, pause them, replay them, and revisit them as and when necessary. In the face-to-face classroom, this opens up more time for questions, guidance, tutorials, student–student interaction, etc.

So what about language teaching? Could we flip our classrooms and would we want to do so? If so, what sort of videos would we create and what sort of content would we deliver? How would we get our students to engage with the videos? Below are some ideas and examples of interactive teacher-produced videos.

Try this ☞ **Giving instructions for a task**

Naturally, teachers will often set homework tasks at the end of a lesson – exactly when students are starting to switch off. If a task is potentially complex and requires more instruction than normal, refer students to a short video in which you explain exactly what you want them to do. An example of this is provided in Video 12.8.

Try this ☞ **Explanations and definitions**

Using English to explain English is a potentially confusing business. And often, students will prefer to stay silent rather than admit failure to understand. With video tools, you can share short presentations with your students, in which you clarify language points and provide illustrative examples. Videos can be made in response to questions that come up in class. Alternatively, they can be made to equip students with language knowledge that they will need for the next class. For this purpose, there are a number of apps such as Educreations (see Appendix 7) that provide a recordable whiteboard that simultaneously captures your voice and handwriting. An example of this is provided in Video 12.9.

Try this 👉 **Today's language**

Through video, we can encourage students to engage with the specific words, phrases, collocations, and structures that they met in a previous class. An example of this is provided in Video 12.10.

✔ *Getting it right*

Start small

Flipping your classroom requires planning videos, creating videos, and implementing new classroom protocols. All of this requires time – something that most teachers are in short supply of. If you are thinking of implementing such a programme or classroom culture you may want to start small and experiment with a single group of students rather than introducing a new approach across the board.

↓ TEACHER DEVELOPMENT

Potentially, one of the greatest beneficiaries of a video camera in the classroom will be you – the teacher. It is true that most of us feel uncomfortable about watching ourselves on video or hearing our voices on audio. However, once we get used to doing so, there is a lot that we can learn from self-observation.

By watching videos of ourselves teaching, we may become aware of our strengths and weaknesses. Video is particularly useful for monitoring our teacher talk and the way in which we interact with students.

It is often said that the single best thing that a teacher can do to develop is to observe other teachers. In situations where that is not a practical option, video-recording devices may be the next best thing. Video is the best medium for capturing and communicating the organic character of the classroom. The written word tells. Video shows.

Glossary

Asynchronous video communication Asynchronous means 'not live'. For example, if students create webcam videos and then share them online for others to respond to, that would involve asynchronous video communication.

Blended learning Any situation in which a face-to-face classroom component is complemented and enhanced with learning technologies. For example, it could involve teacher and students communicating and interacting online as well as in class. It could also involve teacher and students sourcing, creating, sharing, and interacting with online materials such as video.

Blog A blog (or web log) is a website that can be managed by a single person or a group of people. Their popularity is attributed to the fact that they are generally simple to set up and manage. Blogs consist of a series of posts (or entries) that are displayed in reverse chronological order so that the most recent appears first. Blog visitors usually have the option to leave comments. Blogs can be managed at the level of the individual teacher.

Blooper A short video of an unexpected mishap – something going wrong during a live broadcast, for example. Bloopers are often funny, entertaining, and usually associated with television. In the world of user-generated content, the word has been replaced by the term 'fail video'.

Blue/green screens These are pieces of blue or green fabric which create a background for actors or presenters to perform in front of. Later, as a post-production special effect, the blue or green background can be replaced with any image (either moving or non-moving) to give the viewer the impression that the action is taking place somewhere else.

Camcorder A general and familiar term for a video camera. It can be thought of as distinct from other video-recording devices such as smart phones, tablet computers, and webcams.

Chroma key The function in a video-editing application that is used to replace a green or blue background (see *Blue/green screens*) with an image (moving or non-moving) of your choice.

Download When you download a piece of media (an image or video file, for example), you take it off the internet and store it on your own computer.

Dubbing The process of replacing people's voices in a film or video. In the world of cinema, the purpose of dubbing can be to change the spoken language.

Embed By embedding a video on a web page (a VLE, blog, or wiki, for example) you allow visitors to watch the video without leaving the page and going to the site where the video is hosted (YouTube, for example).

Failed video A video in which something unexpectedly goes wrong. The term has emerged through video-sharing culture (as opposed to television) and is often associated with user-generated content.

Flipped classroom A flipped classroom situation (also known as reversed teaching) is one in which students are able to watch videos of teacher-delivered presentations or lectures in their own time. This frees up more face-to-face time for interaction, discussion, collaboration, tasks, etc. The idea originated from contexts involving content-based subjects such as maths. However, there are aspects of the flipped classroom that can be brought to language teaching.

Framing Paying attention to the composition that you see in your shot as you film a video.

Interactive whiteboard An interactive whiteboard (or IWB) is a classroom display surface that may replace or complement a traditional wall-mounted blackboard or whiteboard. Images from a connected computer are projected onto the IWB and the user can control the screen display by touching it directly.

Kinetic typography An animation technique involving moving, onscreen text. The original kinetic typographer was perhaps Saul Bass, who designed the colourful little sequences for the Hitchcock films *North by Northwest* and *Psycho*. In the age of online video, kinetic typography videos have become popular with advertisers and animators, both amateur and professional.

Non-verbal communication Visual cues that contribute towards the construction of meaning from spoken language (gesture, facial expressions, posture, body position, etc.) The importance of cues like these underlines the importance of simultaneous visual and audio as opposed to audio alone.

Offline If you are working offline, you are working without access to the internet.

Online If you are working online, you are working with access to the internet.

Plugin A little piece of software that is added to a larger piece of software to give it a new function. For example, in order to watch YouTube videos online, some internet browsers require the Adobe Flash Player plugin.

Projector By connecting a projector to a computer, the display can be projected onto a white wall or screen in the classroom. The projected image is amplified and this makes it a valuable tool for displaying video to large groups of students.

QR code QR (Quick Response) codes are square two-dimensional barcodes that can be read by mobile devices and link to web pages or short text. In order to read them, the user must download a specialized app for the purpose.

Screencast A video file that captures moving activity on your computer screen. Screencast applications are popular with those who create instructional videos to demonstrate onscreen technological skills (how to use a video-editing application, for example).

Screenshot A screenshot or screen capture can be thought of as a photograph of your computer screen. In order to obtain one, you can make use of a screen capture application. The ability to create images in this way allows you to obtain stills from online videos.

SD card (SD = Secure Digital) The removable memory card inside your digital camera or camcorder which stores your digital photographs or video files.

Stealth advert Any online video advertisement in which the product, brand, or service is not immediately obvious. Stealth videos aim to create online interest, encourage user-interaction, and generate (social) media hype.

Still A still is a non-moving image that is taken from a video. Users can make use of screen capture functions or software to obtain stills from online videos.

Streaming When you watch a video online on a site like YouTube, you stream it. Streaming is usually characterized by a red or blue sliding bar underneath the video window which sometimes gets stuck. Streaming can be contrasted with watching video offline.

Synchronous video communication Synchronous video communication is that which takes place in real time. Synchronous video tools include video chat applications such as Skype.

Upload If you upload a piece of media (an image or video file, for example) you put it on the internet. Uploading a video file usually involves putting it on a video-hosting site such as YouTube.

URL A URL (Uniform Resource Locator) is the address for a specific website, webpage, online video, etc. that appears at the top of your internet browser. For example: http://www.youtube.com/watch?v=9bZkp7q19f0 would be an example of a URL for a YouTube video.

USB (Universal Serial Bus) A standard data-transfer connection that is used to connect a computer to another device such as a memory stick, external hard drive, digital camera, or camcorder.

User-generated Created by everyday people as opposed to traditional mainstream content producers such as TV networks and major film studios.

VGA cable (Video Graphics Array) The standard cable that is used to connect a computer to a projector.

Viral A viral video is an online video that has become popular through the process of internet sharing (emailing, social media, etc.). With 1.8 billion views at the time of writing, Psy's *Gangnam Style* is probably the best-known example of a viral video.

Viral marketing When advertisers make use of social media (Facebook, Twitter, YouTube, etc.) to create a buzz or generate interest for their product, brand, or campaign, this is often called 'viral marketing'.

VLE A virtual learning environment is an online space where teachers and students can interact, share work, and organize online materials (videos, for example). In blended learning situations, the VLE is a digital bridge that connects the online and face-to-face components. VLEs are usually managed at the level of the educational institute.

Vox pop Vox pops (or *vox populi*) are sometimes referred to as 'man or woman on the street' interviews. Vox pop interviews are usually very short. During news broadcasts, they are played in succession, with one interviewee's thoughts following another's.

Webcam A video camera that is connected to your computer for the purpose of video chat, for example. Traditionally, web cams were separate devices that sat above a computer monitor. Modern computers, as well as smart phones and tablets, generally have built-in webcams that allow them to be used as video-recording devices.

Wiki A wiki is a collaborative website that allows a group of people to add, delete, or modify content. Although Wikipedia is the most famous wiki, most are set up for considerably less ambitious projects! For example, a group of students could use a wiki to collaborate and share their work online. Wikis are generally simpler to use and less versatile than VLEs, and can often be managed at the level of the individual teacher.

Appendices

The following abbreviations are used throughout the appendices.

OA: Online application
WS: Website
PC: Downloadable application for PC computers
Mac: Downloadable application for Mac computers
iOS: iPad and/or iPhone app (found at the iTunes app store)
Android Android tablet computer and/or smart phone app (found at Google Play)

↓ APPENDIX 1: FREE SOURCES OF ONLINE VIDEO CONTENT FOR THE CLASSROOM

Archive.org/movies: A non-profit, US-based digital library which offers a lot of downloadable video content, much of it from yesteryear. (WS/iOS/Android)

BigThink.com: Interviews, ideas, and presentations (WS)

Blip.tv: Original web video content and series (WS/iOS/Android)

Dailymotion.com: General content (WS/iOS/Android)

Hulu.com: Mainstream US TV and video content. Only available in the US (WS)

iPlayer.com: BBC video content, only available in the UK. Allows users to download videos for a limited period of time (WS/iOS/Android)

LiveLeak.com: Current events, politics, and caught on camera incidents (WS/Android)

Metacafe.com: General content (WS/iOS)

Movieclips.com: Cinematographic content (WS)

Nationalarchives.gov.uk/films: British video content from yesteryear (WS)

TED.com: Downloadable presentations with multi-language subtitles and transcripts (WS/iOS/Android)

Vevo.com: Music videos (WS/iOS/Android)

Videojug.com: Downloadable 'how to' and instructional videos (WS/Android)

Vimeo.com: Short films, some downloadable (WS/iOS/Android)

YouTube.com: General content (WS/iOS/Android)

To access any of the following channels, run a search of the channel name (shown in **bold**) at YouTube.

Aardman: Animation studio behind *Wallace & Gromit*, *Creature Comforts*, and *Morph*

AlJazeeraEnglish: World news and current affairs

BanksyFilm: British graffiti artist Banksy's channel

BBCEarth: Natural history

BBCWorldwide: Classic BBC clips including comedy, drama, and documentaries

BritainsGotTalent09: British TV talent show contest

Channel4News: British broadcaster

CNN: News and current affairs

Discovery: Discovery Channel – popular science and documentaries

FutureShorts: Short films label

ITNNews: British broadcaster

MontyPython: Classic British comedy series

MuppetsStudio: Classic children's show *The Muppets*

NationalGeographic: Geography, anthropology, natural science

Olympic: The Olympic Games

PESFilm: US animator PES's channel

SciAmerican: *Scientific American* video content

SesameStreet: US children's educational programme

TheGuardian: Video content from the British newspaper

UniversalNewsreels: Content from the pre-television era

YouTube.com: (WS/iOS/Android)

Vimeo.com: A popular alternative to YouTube. The basic package is free, but limits the number of videos that you can upload each week. In order to increase this, you will have to pay a subscription. (WS/iOS/Android)

Photobucket.com: Traditionally a photo-sharing site, Photobucket now hosts video as well. Users must be 17 years of age. (WS/iOS/Android)

SchoolTube.com: A great website for students to host their videos but not very user-friendly to those living and working outside the USA (WS)

Vine: A mobile app that allows you to create and share very short looping videos (the maximum length is 6 seconds). Users must be 17 years of age. (iOS/Android)

Youku.com: With YouTube unavailable in China, this is the country's most popular video-hosting site (WS/iOS/Android)

YouTube is the most popular video-hosting site and also the most versatile. Here are some features that you and your students can make use of.

Annotations: When editing your own videos on YouTube, the annotations feature allows you to add onscreen notes and onscreen links to other videos.

Audioswap: A feature that allows you to find selected Creative Commons music to accompany your videos. The search function allows you to tailor music according to genre, theme, and track length.

Captions: A feature which allows you to add subtitles to your video. It includes an excellent tool for transcribing spoken language.

Improve this video: This is a tool that allows you to add various effects to your video. For example, you can change lighting and colour. You can also stabilize your video (reduce unwanted movements that result from camera shake) and blur out faces to hide identities.

Playlists: The 'Add to' function allows you to bookmark favourite videos and create themed playlists which can be shared or kept private.

Safety mode: At the bottom of the YouTube page, there is a switch that allows you to turn on the safety mode. This hides videos that may contain inappropriate content.

Subscriptions: Subscribe to a channel and select the 'email with new uploads' option. That way, you will receive an email to notify you whenever a new video is uploaded to that channel.

YouTube.com/editor: Allows you to make edits to your own videos as well as videos on the site with a Creative Commons licence.

YouTube.com/education: A sub-section of YouTube which contains curated, high-quality educational video content.

YouTube.com/schools: A network setting that allows school administrators to control the YouTube content that students can access.

YouTube.com/teachers: A 'how-to' site that offers ideas for ways to use YouTube in the classroom.

Blogs

Wordpress.org (PC/Mac/iOS/Android)

Blogger.com (WS/iOS/Android)

It is possible to organize videos on a class blog. However, blogs were never designed to be written by groups of people and may, therefore, be less versatile than other options.

Online pin boards, posters, and walls

Pinterest.com (WS/iOS/Android)

Glogster.com (WS/iOS)

Padlet.com (WS)

Educlipper.net (WS)

Although not particularly versatile, sites like these can be used to create and share online spaces in which multiple videos are displayed in collage-style format. This could be useful for exhibiting or documenting videos based on a theme (all of the videos that you use in class over a term, a series of videos produced by students for a specific project or task, etc.)

Popular VLEs

Edmodo.com (WS/iOS/Android)

Edmodo works very much like Facebook but is designed for schools. Teachers can create groups and invite students to join by providing them with a code. Unlike Facebook, there is a folder system which allows for the organization of content (embedded videos and accompanying materials, for example). This is a great option for teachers whose schools do not have a formal VLE. It is simple to set up and easy to use.

Social media sites

Facebook.com (WS/iOS/Android)

The familiarity of Facebook makes it a contender for a place to post and comment on videos, especially for groups of mature teens and adults. In order to do this, you would have to set up a page or group and invite your students to join. One problem, however, is that the more distant a post or update on Facebook, the more difficult it is to retrieve. This means that Facebook is a particularly bad option if documenting, organizing, and storing videos is a priority.

Wikis

Wikispaces.com (WS)

Sites.Google.com(WS)

A wiki consists of a series of pages to which anyone with permission can add content. Wikis can be effective for organizing videos and allowing for interaction.

↓ APPENDIX 6: SOURCES FOR CREATIVE COMMONS (CC) CONTENT

Commons.wikimedia.org (Wikimedia Commons): A good source of downloadable CC- licensed audio, images, and video.

Flickr.com: This popular photo-sharing website has a search facility that allows users to find images with CC licences.

Freesound.org: A source of CC-licensed sound files containing all sorts of sound effects that could be incorporated into videos.

Search.creativecommons.org: The Creative Commons Organization's own site offers a search function that allows you to find a whole range of CC-licensed media.

Vimeo.com: The site contains a CC search function. Videos with a CC licence can usually be downloaded.

YouTube.com: Use the search filter to find videos with a Creative Commons licence. These can then be edited in the YouTube editor (see Appendix 4).

Appendices

Where possible, the websites, mobile apps, and online applications that are listed here are free. In some cases, however, a one-off payment or a subscription may be necessary.

Animated movie generators

Voki.com (OA)

Dvolver.com/moviemaker (OA)

GoAnimate.com (OA)

PowToon.com (OA)

Xtranormal.com (OA)

These allow you to create animated videos with either automated speech or onscreen text.

Digital storytelling software

Animoto.com (OA)

Microsoft Photo Story (PC)

These allow you to turn a slide show of images into a video file with added audio. Note that presentation software such as Power Point and many image organizers also allow you to do this.

File converter

Zamzar.com (OA) As well as converting video files from one type to another, this online application allows you to convert a video file to an MP3 (audio) file.

File sharing

Dropbox.com (PC/Mac/iOS/Android) This allows you to share video files in a communal online folder.

Media player

VLC player from videolan.org (PC/Mac) This allows you to play otherwise incompatible video files on a communal school computer.

Meme generator

Memecenter.com (OA) Mentioned on page 102.

Presentation software

Prezi.com (OA/iOS/Android) Allows you to:
- create dynamic presentations with embedded videos
- play online videos in class without distractions (adverts, links to suggested videos, etc.)
- play a video and hide its title.

QR codes

Goqr.me (OA) This allows you to create QR codes.

Scan (iOS/Android) This allows QR codes to be read with mobile devices.

Safe video viewing

Safeshare.tv (OA) This allows you to:
- play online videos in class without distractions (adverts, links to suggested videos, etc.),
- change or hide the title of a video.

Screen capture software

Techsmith.com/**jing** (PC/Mac) This allows you to obtain still images from a video.

Screencast software

Techsmith.com/**jing** (PC/Mac)
Camstudio.org (PC)
Educreations.com (OA/iOS)
These allow you to create video recordings of your computer screen and add your voice.

Subtitles

Overstream.net (OA)
Subtitle-horse.com (OA)
Amara.org (OA)
Captiontube.appspot.com (OA)
These allow you to subtitle other people's videos. To subtitle your own videos, you can use a video editor or YouTube (see Appendix 4).

Synchronized notes

Videonot.es (OA) This allows you to write notes while watching a video and then synchronize them with the specific moments to which they refer.

Teleprompters

Prompterous (iOS/Android)
Cueprompter.com (OA)
These are mentioned in Chapter 11.

Video chat

Skype.com (PC/Mac/iOS/Android)
Facetime (Mac/iOS)
Google.com/**Hangouts** (PC/Mac/iOS/Android)
ooVoo.com (PC/Mac/iOS/Android)
These applications allow you to set up synchronous (live) video conversations.

Video discovery sites

Reddit.com/r/videos/
StumbleUpon.com

Bestofyoutube.com

These are mentioned in Chapter 4.

Video downloaders

Zamzar.com (OA)

Torchbrowser.com (OA)

Downloadhelper.net (Firefox browser extension)

Savevid.com (OA)

These allow you to download videos and store them on your computer. Please note that in many cases, this can involve breach of copyright, breach of terms of service, or both. Check with individual websites.

Video editors

Windows Movie Maker (PC)

iMovie (Mac/iOS)

Magisto (Android)

Vidtrim (Android)

Different video editors offer different features and effects. For example, iMovie offers a number of templates to create custom film trailers.

Video remix tools

Metta.io (OA)

Popcorn.webmaker.org (OA)

Touchcast (iOS)

Applications like these allow you to combine your own videos or other people's videos with onscreen text, images, and more. Touchcast allows you to create videos with news-report style onscreen text and graphics and more.

Video search engines

Google.com/video (OA)

Bing.com/video (OA)

These are mentioned in Chapter 4.

↓ APPENDIX 8: OTHER ONLINE RESOURCES FOR TEACHERS

Lessonstream.org: The author's own website. Many plans based on online videos

Film-English.com: Lesson plans around short films by Kieran Donaghy

Nikpeachey.blogspot.com: A good place to find out about the latest video tools for the classroom

TeacherTrainingVideos.com: IT instructional videos for teachers from Russell Stannard.

Digizen.org/cyberbullying: Anti-cyberbullying resources for teachers.

BBC.co.uk/nature: Mentioned in Chapter 7